T0131805

OTHER TITLES IN THE SMART POP SERIES

Ardeur

Ardeur

14 Writers on the Anita Blake, Vampire Hunter Series

◆ ◆ ◆

Edited by Laurell K. Hamilton

With Leah Wilson

An Imprint of BenBella Books, Inc.
Dallas, TX

Smart Pop is an imprint of BenBella Books, Inc.
10440 N. Central Expressway, Suite 800 • Dallas, TX 75231
benbellabooks.com • smartpopbooks.com
Send feedback to feedback@benbellabooks.com

BenBella and Smart Pop are federally registered trademarks.

Printed in the United States of America

Library of Congress Cataloging-in-Publication Data is available for this title.
ISBN 978-1933771-47-2

Some copyediting by Oriana Leckert
Proofreading by Erica Lovett and Gregory Teague
Cover illustration by Ralph Voltz • Cover design by Laura Watkins
Text design and composition by Yara Abuata

Special discounts for bulk sales are available.
Please contact bulkorders@benbellabooks.com.

CONTENTS

I remember the May 2000 Nebula Awards in New York that Nick Mamatas writes about. There was a signing at a Barnes & Noble for the Nebula nominees (the Nebula is a literary award for the Science Fiction Writers of America [SFWA]). I was indeed one of the writers who was also appearing and not a nominee.

Most book signings are bleak. You sit at a little table with your books and people avoid your gaze, as if meeting it means they must buy something, or they think you work for the store. I got that a lot early on. It's one of the reasons I stopped wearing the skirt suits or business casual. I got tired of being asked, "Where are the baseball card books?" I did years of signings like that, and then came this signing.

My agent, Merrilee Heifetz of Writer's House, had showed up to give me moral support. I appreciated that. She alone knew that there were other things on my mind that weekend than networking. The nominees were reading from their works and the rest of us stood to one side quietly listening. Then the first group of women came up the escalator and spotted my name tag. They did that squeal-scream. I admit it scared me. Then they were so excited to see me. It was wonderful, but the other writers were reading, so I did my best to quiet them and assure them I'd sign books after the other writers were done. The second or third time I got that double-take on my name tag, and had to talk to fans while the other writers were still reading, I took my name tag off and gave it to Merrilee to hide. That helped a little, but it was too late, I had been spotted. When time came for the official book signing, Barnes & Noble had to give me a table and a chair of my own to one side, sort of segregated from the other authors, because my line was as big as everyone else's combined. It was the kind of crowd that you want for a signing and never get. It was gratifying and embarrassing. Yay, I was a success. Boo, I worried it would make the other writers feel bad. I had a signing years ago when no one knew who I was, and got to sit by Margaret Weiss when Dragonlance was a very big deal.

I signed maybe two books; her line was gigantic. So I'd been on the other end of the event.

What no one but my agent and my editor at the time knew was that my marriage was over. I was dating again after a decade and change. I had broken up with my current boyfriend just before I got on the plane to New York. The attention of the fans was only part of the change that weekend. At the Nebula dinner, publishers, editors, and other professionals in our business were all over me in a good, happy way. Suddenly I was everyone's golden girl. It had only taken about a decade of writing and publishing to get there.

—*Laurell*

Giving the
Devil Her Due

Why *Guilty Pleasures* Isn't One

NICK MAMATAS

I have a deep respect for Laurell K. Hamilton, which never fails to surprise people. My own fiction is on the "slipstream" edge of the genre, as likely to be published in an underground zine or mainstream literary journal as it is in a genre magazine. My few books have been published by independent presses, some run out of the publishers' apartments, others well-known for their lists of titles about overthrowing the government. Hamilton, of course, is one of the most popular and mainstream of fantasy and horror writers. Surely I should be in the back of a café somewhere, in a black turtleneck and a beret, cursing my own fate and shaking my fist at Hamilton. It's what more than a few of my friends preoccupy themselves with. But I'm not—I think Hamilton, especially in her early books, did some significant work. The Anita Blake series earned its popularity by doing something very little fantasy and horror did in the 1990s: it took women seriously.

This revelation came to me years ago. In May 2000, the Science Fiction and Fantasy Writers of America (SFWA) held their annual Nebula award show and conference in New York City. As part of the weekend, SFWA put on a reading and signing event at the large Barnes & Noble in Union Square. Nebula nominees were invited to read for all of ninety seconds apiece, Grandmaster Brian Aldiss gave a talk, and SFWA members attending the awards showed up. The ads for the event were simple enough: the Nebula nominees got top billing, and there was a long list of writers "also appearing" at the event and available for autographs.

Like most events with lots of writers and relatively few fans, the bookstore smelled of acrid desperation and sounded like a cattle auction. Why so few fans? It's common knowledge that the readership for science fiction and fantasy is "graying"—older men and women still read the stuff, but kids these days are going for anime and video games. The Nebulas, while prestigious in science fiction circles, aren't exactly the Oscars, either. The nominees took their places at the tables the bookstore set up for them, and the "also appearing" writers prowled alone or in small packs, waving bookmarks and cover flats, hoping that someone might recognize them or want a signature. Few people did, for much the same reason few people approach the crazy man who spends his day at the Port Authority passing out leaflets and shouting about sperm, The Book of Revelation, and gravity. It's just creepy.

Then Laurell K. Hamilton showed up. She was very popular, despite being just another writer who was "also appearing." Popular enough that Barnes & Noble employees had to come up with a table and a chair for her, because Laurell K. Hamilton had a *line*, one as long as the Nebula nominees *en masse* had. Rather than the usual suspects of New York's science fiction fandom and the occasional aspiring writer (guilty!), the people in Hamilton's line were quite different. They were women. They were people of color. They had traveled from as far as the Bronx, and sometimes mothers and daughters had even come together. They brought presents for Hamilton—you know, roses and whatnot. They had tons of well-loved and often reread paperbacks with cracked spines for her to sign. Hamilton fans were all smiles, while the people getting signatures from the Nebula nominees tended to have the eagerly blank look often sported by the professional fan or the resigned mugs of an eBay "power seller" looking for a score.

Science fiction and fantasy people—writers, editors, publishers, Big Name Fans, you name it—have spent years bemoaning declining readership. It's too old, it's not being replenished by kids, there's not enough stuff that appeals to women and to people of color. Hamilton changed all that, even before she became a bestselling author. A look at *Guilty Pleasures*, the first of the Anita Blake novels, can help us understand the level of Hamilton's achievement. With Blake and the universe she inhabits—one in which vampires have Supreme Court protections—Hamilton accomplished the seemingly impossible: she created a new subgenre, urban fantasy-adventure with a female lead, and built a new audience for it. Here is how she did it.

1. Hamilton Realized That Female Readers Want a Kick-Ass Heroine They Can Identify With

Anita Blake has few female antecedents in popular literature. If anything, Blake is a character straight out of Robert Howard, except that she has a vulnerability and an honesty that few "badasses" do. Here she is reminiscing in *Guilty Pleasures* about being attacked by a vampire, one she is confronting again:

> My screams. His hand forcing my head back. Him rearing
> to strike. Helpless. . . . He lapped up my blood like a cat
> with cream. I lay under his weight listening to him lap up
> my blood. . . . I was beginning not to hurt, not to be afraid.
> I was beginning to die.

Who saves Anita? Anita does, with holy water that had fallen from her bag. She doesn't kill the vampire, but scars him for eternity. And Anita wears plenty of scars, too, displaying them like badges of honor to her enemy. In 1993, this was powerful stuff. It may be difficult, in these post-*Buffy* times, to remember quite how revolutionary Anita was just seventeen years ago. In virtually any other novel of the period, Anita's boyfriend—or even worse, a man she loathed but whom she could not help but be attracted to—would have saved her. The fangs on her neck would have been a recurring theme throughout the novel, indeed perhaps even throughout the series, as the author reveled in the rape survivor–like vulnerability of the "heroine." Hamilton didn't play that way, and was not afraid to show us Blake's fear and her bravery, her interest in justice and her own interior darkness.

2. Hamilton Didn't Shy Away From, or Romanticize, the Sex

Sex is a part of life, but if one reads romance novels, sex is either too dirty to contemplate or too comical to enjoy: purple-helmeted warriors of love and all that. In science fiction and fantasy, the situation was even worse—the genres were essentially celibate. Outliers such as Anne Rice, who had long before left the genre and has simply become a Bestselling Author, had plenty of sexuality, but much of it was inhuman or involved no women. Hamilton, through Blake's eyes, had a sense of sex and the physical details of the body that readers wanted. Here's a great scene from *Guilty Pleasures*:

> She pulled down the silky bra to expose the upper mound of her breast. There was a perfect set of bite marks in the pale flesh. . . . I thought he was going to ask for help, but she kissed him, sloppy and deep, like she was drinking him from the mouth down. His hands began to lift the silk folds of her skirt. Her thighs were incredibly white, like beached whales.

Perhaps this was the first time in the history of dark fantasy that the words "breast" and "perfect" were used in close proximity to one another without perfect being used to describe the breast in question. Kisses are sloppy and thighs like beached whales—not lines to use on one's lover in bed!—yet there is a strong sensuality in the books anyway. Vampires are both superhuman and subhuman, objects of desire and creepy monsters. In that way, they are much like human beings—in the whirl of sex, even flaws and rolls of fat take on an attractive mien. While not often appreciated for this, Hamilton's early books are both highly sexual and realistic. Rather than appealing to the high Romantic notions of the vampire popularized by Rice, Hamilton performed a little nucleic exchange between the woman's novel, the vampire story, and the noir mystery. Sex was as fun as it was dirty in Hamilton's narrative universe, and after more than a decade of treacle and misdirection, readers were ready for a heroine who couldn't say "make love" with a straight face.

Interestingly enough, in *Guilty Pleasures*, Blake herself doesn't have sex. The tag line of the 1993 paperback even reads, "I don't date vampires, I kill them." However, the world remains a sensuous, sexualized one. The abject—the idea of simultaneous attraction and revulsion—is in play, and this notion is essential to good vampire stories. Turn the vampires into shambling subhuman monsters, and you may as well be watching a zombie film. Make them Fabio-style romance heroes with pirate sleeves and six-pack abs, and there's no terror in the monster. Hamilton struck a middle ground in *Guilty Pleasures* in an intriguing way, with a heavily sexualized setting and a non-sexual protagonist.

3. Blake Has Real Problems

Popular fiction is full of what writer and teacher Stace Budzko calls "Cowboy problems." The everyday issues and problems we all face simply don't show up amidst all the world-saving and bad guy–shooting that paperbacks occupy themselves with. Indeed, this strange divorce from real life is part of why books chock full of death, beatings, torture, war, privation, and horrors are "escapes" for their readers.

Anita Blake has real problems, though. After raising a zombie, she runs for it and falls on her ass. "Hose are not made for running in," she notes. Of course the zombie isn't the real problem; the lack of traction in the pantyhose is. The taste of realism, and Blake's matter-of-fact remark, help us to actually believe in the fantastical problem of being chased by a zombie. And here's a problem that everyone has faced one weekend morning or other:

> The alarm shrieked through my sleep. It sounded like a car alarm, hideously loud. I smashed my palm on the buttons. Mercifully, it shut off. I blinked at the clock through half-slit eyes. Nine a.m. Damn. I had forgotten to unset the alarm. I had time to get dressed and make church. I did not want to get up. I did not want to go to church. Surely, God would forgive me just this once.

There is a near-inevitable scene in fantasy books, and more than a few crime novels, where someone "gears up." A wise old figure hands out the magical devices, or offers up sufficient money, outfits, and limos to make a private dick look like he's made good. Not Anita. She spends the early novels slogging through a world where she is outclassed in virtually every way. While she has significant internal resources and some vampire-related powers she suffered to gain, she is also an ordinary woman of ordinary means, a small-time player punching *way* out of her weight class. It's how we all feel sometimes, in this world of pointy-haired managers and rich Hollywood types who can get away with behavior that would see us disowned, arrested, or even just beaten down on the streets. No maids, no gadgets, no perfect life disrupted by the supernatural—Anita was a bit of a mess to begin with, adding a level of verisimilitude not seen in previous heroines, or even in many of the subsequent urban fantasy novels in the Blake mode. No less of an authority on the fantastic than Italo Calvino explained it best: "Fantasy is like jam. . . . You have to spread it on a solid piece of bread. If not, it remains a shapeless thing . . . out of which you can't make anything." Blake's quotidian problems are the crust on which the fantasy lays, and what makes the fantasy feel realistic enough to work. Most contemporary urban fantasy has not learned this lesson.

4. Male Characters Are Somewhat Idealized, but Have to Work to Keep Up with the Female Lead

Movies, TV shows, and novels often portray women as making themselves over in order to attract an inaccessible man, a "Prince Charming." Indeed, there is a whole category of romance novel known as the "makeover novel." Anita Blake, on the other hand, ain't down with makeovers. She's tough, and makes the men work for her, or triumphs over them. Sometimes this happens in small ways. Coming across a woman in "sheer black stockings held up by garter belts" and a bra/panty set in royal purple, walking along in five-inch spiked heels, inspires Anita to declare:

"I'm overdressed."

"Maybe not for long," [Phillip] breathed into my hair.

"Don't bet your life on it." I stared up at him as I said it and watched his face crumble into confusion.

Phillip recovers a moment later, and Anita worries about what she has gotten herself into. But she does triumph, and not only in the end. In a standard fantasy novel, there might be some of this sort of repartee in the early chapters, but only to signal to the reader that by the end of the book the heroine will be in the hero's bed and ready for a life of non-threatening monogamous domestic-sexual bliss. Attractive and sexually available men weren't allowed to lose to women in popular fiction, not for long anyway. Even if a woman triumphed over a man intellectually, economically, or rhetorically in a scene or two, by the end of the book the female lead would be humbled and ready to submit to the male lead. Hamilton changed that. Blake calls the shots with her relationships in *Guilty Pleasures* and continues to remain the ultimately dominant partner across much of the series.

Despite the fact that women buy the majority of books published in the United States, it is easy for publishers, editors, and writers to not take women seriously. "Women's fiction," romance, and other genres—whether read primarily by men or by women—are disreputable, designed to be disposable. The mass market paperback market is treated like a dumping ground for books fit only to be bought on a whim at supermarkets and airports. This is pretty easy to see from *Guilty Pleasures*—the original cover art in the paperback was downright cartoonish, looking more like an R. L. Stine book than a hard-boiled novel. Blake is not even the size of the male character's nose, and the logo for the series is strongly reminiscent of Batman's chest emblem. There's even an entirely inexplicable back cover blurb from Andre Norton, assuring the reader that while *Guilty Pleasures* is "a departure from the usual type of vampire tale," the book is still full of "chills and fun." Yes. Chills, fun, and a revolution in popular fiction.

The women's mass market is not where publishers expect to find new audiences or, for that matter, new genres. Yet Laurell K. Hamilton did exactly that in 1993 with the publication of *Guilty Pleasures*. While the "serious" writers of the genre spent much of the last decade fuming at those dumb audiences and their taste for kiddy books like Harry Potter or video games, Hamilton showed that fantasy could reach a new and powerful audience of women. All it took was a new and powerful woman character: Anita Blake.

◆   ◆   ◆

Nick Mamatas is the author of two novels—*Move Under Ground* and *Under My Roof*—and over fifty short stories, some of which have recently been collected in *You Might Sleep.* . . . His fiction has been nominated for the Bram Stoker and International Horror Guild awards and as editor of the online magazine *Clarkesworld*, Nick has been nominated for both the Hugo and World Fantasy awards.

When I started writing Anita Blake over a decade ago I was a devout Episcopalian, married to the man I lost my virginity to, and whose virginity I took as well. If I had enough self-control to wait then why would I settle for a man who couldn't be as strong (or that was my thinking at the time)? I totally bought the white-picket-fence soulmate ideal. I was puzzled by people asking me why Anita didn't have sex in the early books. (Yes, once I got flack for keeping Anita out of people's beds. I just can't win on this subject.) Anita didn't have sex because I believed sincerely that you should wait for marriage.

Then a funny thing happened, my soulmate and I turned out to be not so compatible. I had questions that my priest couldn't answer for me. I'd bought the promise of Prince Charming—though I did consider myself Princess Charming rather than the maiden to be rescued, that was never my gig—and the prince turned out to be a nice guy, and I was a nice girl, but two nice people don't always make a good marriage. Two bad people make a worse one, but oddly both types of marriages often end in the same place: divorce.

One of the problems from the beginning for my ex and I was sex. We were virgins so we didn't know what we liked in the bedroom, but the idea that we'd grow together and find our way to happiness didn't quite work out. Sometimes you find that one half of the couple likes meat and potatoes and the other half likes something a little more exotic. Then what? You're married, you've promised to be monogamous, and you don't like the same kind of sex. Because it is different from person to person, and anyone who tells you different is doing it wrong, or badly. Every lover is a new country to explore and he or she can bring out things in you that you never even dreamed could be inside you.

But back to that whole monogamy thing. I lasted over a decade, to my separation when my first husband suggested we both date other people. It was hard to write about Anita finally sleeping with Jean-Claude when my own sex life was not so good, but it was much harder to write about her falling in love with Richard Zeeman, werewolf and all-around Boy Scout. Writing about her love being fresh and new in that way that makes you think anything is possible while the love of my life was ending was one of the most painful things I'd ever done. *Blue Moon*, where Anita finally admits how she feels about Richard, was a very difficult write for me. By the time *Obsidian Butterfly* came out and hit the *New York Times* list, the first of my books to do that, I was either divorced, or on my way, and was out of my house, in a small apartment with my daughter, and on my own for the first time in my adult life. I was also dating for the first time since college and that was interesting. Times had changed and men seemed to assume that a first date with a nice dinner was a guarantee of sex. I actually told one guy who was being less than subtle, "Sure I'll have dinner with you as long as you understand that the price of dinner is not the price of my virtue." He lost one point for not understanding what I said, and all his points for not wanting the date then. I wanted to have sex, good sex, but somehow I didn't feel that most of the men wanting to take me out were going to be good. I wanted good, and wasn't settling for less.

I would finally find it. I would finally not be able to say that I'd only been with one man, or even with two. I began to figure out what I wanted, and what good meant to me in the bedroom and on any other flat surface that would hold the weight. Most tables will not, just a caution. I still haven't done everything I write about, sorry to disappoint, but unlike Anita I haven't yet met that many men I like and trust yet. I am married again, but we lived together for six months first at my insistence. I was not going to make the same mistake twice. I knew exactly what I was getting this time, no unpleasant surprises. He knew what he was getting into, I made sure of that. I didn't want any buyer's remorse in my second marriage.

While I was rebuilding my life I was still writing Anita. If my first marriage had worked would Anita have stayed a "good girl"?

Would she have gone off into the sunset with Richard and the series gone down a more traditional "romance" path? I don't know. I know that it continues to amaze me that being a woman who likes sex and writes about a woman who likes and enjoys sex still shocks people in the United States. Europe, not so much—they have more problems with the violence—but in the good ol' US of A I am still asked to defend my choices as a woman and as a writer.

I love that Heather Swain compared Anita to Bertha from *Jane Eyre*, and Britney Spears. I so wouldn't have thought of that comparison myself, but I like even more her point that where both of the other women lose power through becoming sexual beings, Anita gains power. My grandmother wouldn't let me bring Jonathon home to meet her before we married. I was a fallen woman to her. No, really. But I knew I hadn't fallen, I'd escaped, not my first marriage but the box that I'd tried to fit myself inside for that marriage. Escaped the expectations of what made a woman "good," and what made her a "bad" girl. Ever notice that you're a "good woman," but a "bad girl"? Because the moment you own your sexuality, society still tries to make you less. You're not a woman anymore, you're just a girl. The idea seems to be that you'll grow up, learn the error of your ways, and then you'll be a woman again, a good one. Well, I have grown up, and so has Anita, and we're both just fine the way we are, being not good women, but good people.

—*Laurell*

Girls Gone Wild

Britney, Bertha, and Anita Blake
(How a Southern Virgin, a Fallen Angel, and
an Abstinent Vampire Slayer Became Depraved Women)

HEATHER SWAIN

A good story demands transformation, and for Protestant America's buck, not much beats virtuous Christian girls tumbling into depravation. The mother/whore, the fallen angel, the good girl gone bad rivets readers to the page. When the preacher's daughter winds up the pregnant homecoming queen (or for that matter, the vice-presidential nominee's knocked-up teen stands hand in hand with her hunky beau at the Republican National Convention), only the most enlightened don't snicker behind curled fingers. Even though most modern women think of themselves as liberated and in control of their bodies and libidos, society still has a penchant for demonizing those of the fairer sex who slide down the slope from virgin to sexualized woman. The sweeter the girl and the farther her fall, the better. It's enough to make a girl ask, Can't I just like sex?

The fall of a good woman is a tale that's kept the printing presses churning for centuries, yet there's always a deeper story. If you look past all those flaky flashers on the *Girls Gone Wild* infomercials, you just might find a narrative about the precarious balance of power, sex, and gender politics that has followed women from the Old Testament to *US Weekly* and everything in between—including the Anita Blake series by Laurell K. Hamilton.

At the beginning of Hamilton's series, Anita Blake is a twenty-seven-year-old celibate Christian with a strict moral code about how to use her abilities as a necromancer. Despite her prickly attitude, Anita is a champion for the little guy, even if that guy happens to be a monster sometimes. As she reminds readers over and over again, no matter how much it may rankle her, non-humans have rights in her world. In her work animators frequently cross the line and use their abilities for ill-gotten gains, but Anita balks. She has no problem raising the dead for a profit or killing someone (or something), but only if there's a good reason. And for Anita, that reason is often that if she doesn't, someone innocent will get hurt.

We know that Anita was engaged a few years back but got burned when her fiancé's mother turned out to be a closet racist who didn't want a half-Mexican daughter-in-law. The relationship ended badly and Anita swore off sex before marriage. While her Christian beliefs inform much of her moral code, Biblical doctrine isn't the underpinning for Anita's stance on premarital sex. Her Christianity has more to do with demarcating herself from the monsters that she kills. Anita believes in an afterlife that holds more promise than earthly immortality and the only way to get to the afterlife is through death. But—as anyone who's read beyond book ten, *Narcissus in Chains*, knows—eventually all of that changes and Anita Blake ends up as far from celibate or married (or Heaven, for that matter) as Britney Spears is.

There are cultural doomsayers who like to believe women such as Anita and the popularity of the stories about them are a problem of the modern age, but that's nostalgia for you. Some of the stodgiest classics that high schoolers slog through today were the most scandalous literature of their era. Critics dismissed Jane Austen as fluff, accused the Brontës of being coarse, and Simone de Beauvoir may as well have written porn for all the flack she took.

One of the most enduring depraved women in English literature is Bertha Mason, from Charlotte Brontë's novel *Jane Eyre*.

By the time plain Jane shows up as the governess for Edward Rochester's illegitimate French ward, Adele, she has learned to temper her inner raging woman. This is in stark contrast to Rochester's wife Bertha—his brown sugar mama, who beguiled him with her seductive Creole charm then became a raving lunatic when he brought her back from Jamaica to the civilized world of merry old England where women were expected to submissively devote themselves to their husband's every need. Now (unbeknownst to Jane) Bertha spends her days locked in an attic, guarded by a drunken maid, Grace Poole, who is equally pissed at the world but chooses to drown her sorrows in a pint of ale rather than go mad.

One could read *Jane Eyre* as a warning to women who refuse to acquiesce to their husband's power. Rochester claims Bertha is "intemperate and unchaste," a "lunatic" both "cunning and malignant." He further explains away Bertha's condition as hereditary. Seems her mother and grandmother lost their marbles back in Jamaica. But I'm not buying it. Once Jane and Rochester reveal their love for one another, Bertha acts far too lucidly for a lunatic, no matter how cunning. After Rochester proposes to Jane, Bertha escapes the attic and enters Jane's bedroom, where she places Jane's wedding veil on her own head, then flings it to the ground and tramples it. Whether this is Bertha's way of warning Jane to stay away from Edward because he's bad news for women or a warning for Jane to steer clear of Bertha's man (she is still Edward's wife, after all) is anybody's guess. Either way, Bertha's behavior hardly seems maniacal. Rochester brushes off the incident by blaming poor, drunken Grace Poole.

(It's amusing to imagine at this point that literary worlds could collide. What if Anita were plopped down into *Jane Eyre* as Jane herself? First off, Bertha probably would've had her ass whooped for trampling the veil, and secondly, I doubt Anita/Jane would have taken Rochester's crap. She'd have had him in some judo hold until he admitted the truth. But this is not the case. If anything, Anita has much more in common with Bertha.)

Bertha's brother is the one who stops Jane and Rochester's wedding, by revealing the existence of Bertha. Seems polygamy was frowned upon in England then as now. However, even after the wedding is called off, Rochester tries to persuade Jane to become his mistress (thus tempting her through the door of depravity). To woo Jane, Rochester says she is just what he's been searching for—the "antipodes of Creole." Nice guy—sexist and racist, to boot.

An alternate reading posits that Brontë used Bertha Mason to illustrate what happens when women repress their rage for too long.
Bertha's not the only angry woman in the novel, but she's the one
who lost it all by becoming volatile. Bertha's volatility flew in the face
of the prevailing Victorian notion of the good wife popularized by
Coventry Patmore's 1854 poem "Angel in the House," which extolled
the virtues of a wife who was meek, self-sacrificing, and pure. Bertha
was none of those things, plus she was mad as hell. As the feminist
scholar Jane Anderson points out, "to be an angry woman in nineteenth-century England is next-door to insanity."[1] Rochester believes
Bertha is crazy, but he also links her condition to her lack of chastity.
Seems there's no room in Victorian England for a woman who gets
mad and likes to fuck. Anita wouldn't have stood a chance back then.
They'd have locked her up and called her crazy.

Like most female novelists of her day, Brontë wrote under a pen
name, Currer Bell, to disguise her gender. Reviews of *Jane Eyre* were
quite favorable when critics believed a man had written it. But when
Currer was revealed to be Charlotte, the criticism turned ugly. A re-
viewer for the *Rambler* skewered Brontë for her "relapse into that
class of ideas, expressions, and circumstances, which is most connected with the grosser and more animal portion of our nature." In
other words, she had the audacity and poor taste to allude to sex. Not
only could women not like to *do it* without mental illness to blame,
they couldn't even write about women who might.

Since Anita Blake is an incarnation of the late twentieth-century,
Hamilton probably didn't think she'd have to worry about such prig-
gish reviewers. And at first, sex wasn't an issue because Anita remains
celibate for six books. Not even the super hot Master of the City, vampire Jean-Claude, causes Anita to swoon—which is saying something
because Jean-Claude oozes sex. This is not unlike Jane refusing to
become Rochester's mistress. Both Jane and Anita base their refusals
on morality. For Jane, her Christian beliefs dictate that sex outside
of marriage is a sin. For Anita, her desire to attain a Christian afterlife stops her from bedding a vampire. Anita, unlike Jane, might not

---

[1] Quoted in "Angry Angels: Repression, Containment, and Deviance, in Charlotte Brontë's
Jane Eyre," by Joan Z. Anderson.

believe she'd go to Hell for premarital sex, but she does worry that once she crosses the line from human to monster, she might lose her ability to die and therefore lose her place in Heaven.

Rochester is Brontë's Byronic Man—the kind of guy Lord Byron's ex-lover Lady Caroline Lamb described as "mad, bad and dangerous to know." And Jane is madly in love with him, but she won't compromise her hard-earned virtue. Anita feels similarly about Jean-Claude, although instead of love she feels pure lust. Maybe Jane and Anita could have a support group for Women Who Run with Wolves . . . and Vampires . . . and Werewolves, too.

Later, when Anita falls in love with hunky, thoughtful Richard (who just happens to be a werewolf), she keeps her pants on. It's one thing for her to turn down a vampire. She knows that getting involved with Jean-Claude necessarily means she'll wind up his human servant and then it's bye-bye afterlife. But for Anita to turn down the man she loves unless they're married is some seriously Victorian thinking. Richard doesn't mind, though; he simply asks Anita to marry him. And Anita says yes. At first. Until she says no, that is, and eventually gets involved with both Jean-Claude and Richard. Ah, the tumble begins!

Creating stories about women's chastity and the lack thereof isn't only the providence of novelists. A whole genre of fiction is devoted to rewriting the sexual history of female celebrities. Real life offers plenty of good girls gone bad to captivate mass audiences. How else would the paparazzi stay in business? Every era has its Jezebels; the twenty-first century simply has more media outlets to cover degradation. And Britney Spears has been covered in every one of them.

As Vanessa Grigoriadis points out in her 2008 *Rolling Stone* article "The Tragedy of Britney Spears," Britney was "created as a virgin to be deflowered before us, for our amusement." Once Britney left Disney's *Mickey Mouse Club*, she signed on with manager Larry Rudolph, who promoted seventeen-year-old Britney as a Southern good girl with just a hint of Lolita thrown in to titillate. This version of Britney's life claimed that she was a virgin and planned on saving herself for marriage, even as she dated teen heartthrob Justin Timberlake. Spears' mother, Lynn, debunked that myth years later in her tell-all book,

Through the Storm, in which she claimed Britney lost her virginity at fourteen to her high school boyfriend and that she routinely slept with Timberlake. This from her own mother!

Britney has more in common with Bertha Mason and Anita Blake than you might think. Some speculate the reasons for Britney's unchaste behavior (both in and out of the sack) could be hereditary. Her grandmother was thought to have been mentally ill, as evidenced by shooting herself on the grave of her dead son, pulling the trigger of a shotgun with her big toe. Anita has her own issues of maternal heredity, probably gaining her innate powers of necromancy from her mother's mother, who was a voodoo queen. But there could also be an alternate reading to the Britney Spears story. Like Bertha, Britney is raging against a world that tried to pin her into a tightly circumscribed role. As Grigoriadis says, Britney "doesn't want anything to do with the person the world thought she was." Her current image as a paparazzi-baiting, drug-abusing, head-shaving, midriff-baring sex kitten is about as far from a good Southern girl as Britney could get. And like Bertha, in the process of losing her mind Britney lost nearly everything else in her life—her marriage to Kevin Federline failed, she lost custody of her children, and she's gone in and out of rehab.

Anita is no stranger to rage either, but in her case wrath is a job skill. Anita is able to channel her anger into something productive—killing monsters. Plus, she's the only one of these three women who's licensed to carry a gun. Being a pissy woman who's allowed to shoot bad guys—without punishment—is one of the reasons Anita is so fun to read. Bertha eventually exacts her revenge on Rochester by setting fire to his estate, but while Rochester loses his sight and one hand while fighting the fire, Bertha dies engulfed in the hell-like blaze. Britney's rage is the most impotent of the three because it hurts nobody but herself (and possibly her children, who've, at least for now, lost their mother).

Also like Britney, Anita was set up for her big fall. By making Anita Christian to distinguish her from the monsters, Hamilton allows her to plummet from grace when she finally becomes Jean-Claude's lover. Britney's damnation may not be eternal (there's always next year's VMA Awards) but by accepting Jean-Claude's marks, Anita gives up the one thing she held dear: her chance at a Christian afterlife. But unlike Britney and Bertha, Anita has an out and that out is power.

Where neither Bertha nor Britney could find a toe hold in the world that shaped them and their rage, Anita takes control. She enters a triumvirate with Richard and Jean-Claude in which the vampire, animal servant, and human servant are linked and share power. In turn, Anita becomes Jean-Claude's human servant (thus accepting potential immortality) so the messy doctrine of eternal life via Christianity is out of the way. This doesn't mean that Anita no longer considers herself a Christian, just that she doesn't consider all the sex she's having to be immoral because she's no longer concerned about mortality and an afterlife in a Christian Heaven. In other words, Anita has chosen to play by new rules.

As a consequence of joining forces with Jean-Claude, Anita is infected with the *ardeur*. If mental illness is what drove Bertha and Britney over the edge, the *ardeur* is what makes Anita change from celibate to swinger, and unlike insanity (in Bertha and Britney's cases), this gives her more power, not less. In order to keep the *ardeur* in check, Anita must have several lovers or the *ardeur* will drain her, possibly killing her. She leaves Richard and shacks up with two wereleopards, plus takes on many other lovers to feed her need—sex every six hours. At this point, Anita has to fuck to live.

Here's where Anita's story trumps Bertha and Britney's. When Hamilton gives Anita a reason to go hog wild with sex, she allows the line between human and monster to blur. Anita gains empathy for the creatures she hunts because she's able to see her own will to survive a difficult and unjust world reflected in their lives. Anita says herself, "One of my favorite things about hanging out with the monsters is the healing. Straight humans seemed to get killed on me a lot. Monsters survived. Let's hear it for the monsters" (*Cerulean Sins*). Not only does Anita accept that monsters may have something over humans, but physically she now harbors strains of lycanthrope which may eventually lead to her becoming a shapeshifter. Not only does Anita change from a celibate woman to a highly sexualized being, but her very nature shifts. The fall is complete, but unlike her literary and real-life predecessors, Anita's tumble doesn't undo her. It only makes her stronger.

Gender politics, sex, and power have long been linked in literature and in life, but few characters have had as much fun with them as Anita Blake. In the end, Anita didn't need a man to rescue her from depravity. Hamilton said herself that she set out to write a strong female protagonist who got to do the things men usually get to do in hard-boiled detective novels: kill people without remorse and have lots of sex. Without someone giving them the same permission to live life like a man, Bertha and Britney both crashed and burned, but Anita embraces her depravity as a form of power and has a hell of a good time on her way down.

When Hamilton started the Anita Blake series, she felt there remained a prevailing notion in society that women should not be comfortable, let alone bold, about their sexuality and desire. But over the course of sixteen novels, Hamilton questioned that presumption and slowly shifted Anita into a woman who was both comfortable and bold.

This move has won Anita Blake millions of fans (as evidenced by the number of weeks she's lounged around the *New York Times* bestseller list over the past fifteen years). Britney has retained her wild popularity in spite of, or perhaps because of, her ups and downs, but her "fans" seem to find pity in and fascination for her plight. They laud her accomplishments, but also stand in line to watch her stumble. Bertha's most enduring readers tend to be feminist scholars who look for historical clues about the changing nature of womanhood via literature. Anita fans are different.

Hamilton has taken a fair amount of flack (from critics and fans) for turning Anita books into soft-core monster porn, yet she retains a huge devout group of fans who don't simply read about Anita's exploits, they look to her for life lessons. She's a rare female character who's dangerous and can also take care of herself. She rarely relies on a man to save her tail, but if it turns out that way, she returns the favor in kind later. Although we don't live in world of vampires and werebeasts, real women face their own demons, and according to Hamilton some female fans have left abusive relationships because they said they knew Anita wouldn't take treatment like that.

So this begs the question: is Anita another fallen woman whose popularity hinges on our collective love for watching women tumble? Not in my book. Hamilton wrote new rules for the female protagonist. She could be tough, she could be sexy, she could even be bitchy. She could do whatever she needed to protect herself and make herself happy. I think Anita continues to appeal because, far from falling, she soars.

❖   ❖   ❖

Heather Swain is the author of the young adult novels *Me, My Elf and I* and *Selfish Elf Wish* as well as two novels for adults (*Eliot's Banana* and *Luscious Lemon*), personal essays, magazine articles, and short stories. She lives in Brooklyn, New York, with her husband and two young children, but you can stop by her website www.heatherswainbooks.com anytime for a visit.

First, I hate ambiguity. It's one of my least favorite things. Most of the time, I would rather have a firm no than a maybe. A no means I can move on, a maybe traps me in that gray area between yes and no. That being one of my personality traits, it was inevitable that the dance of *will Anita sleep with, or kill, Jean-Claude?* was going to be answered. I actually set it up to kill him at the end of book three, *Circus of the Damned*, but when the moment came Anita would have missed him, and so would I. The kiss-me-kill-me paradigm can only interest me so long and then I want a choice. People seem to think that Anita not choosing one of the men is ambiguity, but it's not. The choice Anita made was not to pick a single man to be monogamous with, and I'm still taking heat for that particular choice. It certainly wasn't the original plan, but if your first plan doesn't work, make a new one, and keep doing that until something works.

Second, one of the reasons that Anita Blake came on the scene guns blazing and gender roles be damned was that I didn't know how to be a girl. My grandmother raised me to be the boy. It was more important how much I could lift and how hard I could work than what I looked like. What I could do mattered more than how I appeared. I was never, ever told that I should be a soft, feminine, nurturing, passive recipient of any male action. I was raised on stories of my grandfather abusing my grandmother for the twenty years of their marriage. My own biological father had left my mother and they were divorced by the time I was six months old. Men were no good, according to my grandmother, and I didn't need one. I found as I got older it was more fair to say that not all people are good, regardless of their gender, and that though I didn't need a man in a traditional role in my life I did want a man in my life if he could be a true life partner. I always wanted a partner, an equal. Even though my first husband and I divorced he never treated me as less-than because I was a woman, except for a memorable lapse when some male friends convinced him he needed to be the head of the household. I soon let him know that if I couldn't be equal, I wanted nothing to do with him. He backpedaled and never brought it up again. Some things you do not compromise on and being an equal in my marriage was one of them.

Growing up I saw a lot of things. I saw that soft women were victims. I saw that seemingly strong women fell in love and lost their gumption and folded into some feminine ideal that made them victims. Nurturing is good, but I demanded my first husband help with our daughter, and when he had another lapse during my pregnancy with her I told him this: "If you force me to raise our baby like I'm a single parent, I will be." I meant it, he knew it, and he has been a devoted father ever since.

I did not even know that there was an entire girl culture I was clueless about until just a year or so ago, when other women were trying to convince me that I should feel intimidated by a new friend who happened to be tall, blond, blue-eyed, voluptuous, and gorgeous. I didn't understand why I was supposed to be intimidated by my friend. One female business associate explained, patiently, that I should be jealous, or competitive, with my friend. I asked, "Why? She's my friend. The rain is wet and she's beautiful. Why should that bother me?" She never could explain it to me, but later that business trip she showed me: by sandbagging me before an important business dinner. I did the guy thing, and asked her if I needed to dress up for the event. She assured me that business clothes were fine.

When I arrived at the event, I was the only woman there not dressed to kill. Cocktail dresses or more, full make-up, professionally styled hair—the works. The woman herself was in a semi-formal sequined number with her hair done up on top of her head in elaborate curls. In that moment, I got it. I'd intimidated her because I was attractive by her standards and she'd feared that if I dressed up I'd look better than she did. I got that she'd lied to me so I wouldn't look as dressed up. I was the most casually dressed woman there. Did it bother me? Yes, because I hate being lied to.

Did it make me feel less of a woman by wearing something that wasn't as frilly? No. I wasn't competing with anyone at the business function. I was there for business, not to see who could be queen bitch. But this one incident explained a lifetime of mystery regarding other women, and before that other girls, to me. I had been on the receiving end of things like this my whole life and never understood that most of the other women were playing by this secret game, one that I had never been told existed.

I'm only competitive with myself and with people I see as true competition in business. But not in the cutthroat way, only, *How is that writer doing better than me? What are they doing that I'm not?* Who's making more money? Find out how. More prestige? Find out how. I've always looked around and found the writers doing better than me in some way and tried to find out their business plan and do my own version of it. I play to win the big picture, not the small squabbles, but I also play like I believe a woman is "supposed" to play if she really were the kinder sex. I like to see everyone succeed. I'm helpful if I can be. I have never knowingly undercut another woman personally, or in business, just because she was a woman and I felt she might look better than me in a dress. That kind of thinking hurts not only the woman who's being picked on, but even more the woman doing it. The female business associate who was so intimidated by me lost a chance to be my friend, and I try to be a really good friend.

I'm still very good friends with my tall, gorgeous, blond, blue-eyed friend. She and I get along just fine.

—*Laurell*

Ambiguous Anita

LILITH SAINTCROW

One doesn't have to precisely *blame* Laurell K. Hamilton for the explosion of paranormal romance and kickass-chick urban fantasy currently filling bookstore shelves. Hamilton started out, a decade or so ago in *Guilty Pleasures*, with the same type of urban-fantasy-with-a-touch-of-noir that has been a small, important subsection of fantasy ever since someone first decided to cross a detective story with something supernatural. From Wilkie Collins and Bram Stoker (*Dracula* is, after all, a detective story as well as a psychosexual morality play) to Charles de Lint and Simon Green, the supernatural detective is alive and well—for which I am profoundly grateful.

What separated Anita Blake, Vampire Executioner, from the common run of schlock and fantasy was two things: Anita's gender and Anita's ambiguity. I don't think I'm far wrong in stating that Anita was one of the very first "kickass" female characters in urban fantasy, a template for all those ladies with tramp-stamp tattoos and tight clothing hanging out on so many covers nowadays. However, she was not *the* first, and her popularity has its roots in a different dynamic: the fact that Anita Blake is one of the first female protagonists with the noir hallmark of moral and ethical ambiguity guiding her actions.

The phenomenon I refer to as "ambiguous Anita" only shows up in the first five books of the series. By the sixth she is embroiled in a process of becoming a more standard female character, whose primary concern is her interpersonal relationships with the monsters she is embroiled with sexually. This is where Anita loses significant amounts of her noir-ish features: ethical/moral flexibility, dilemmas with no clear "winning" outcome, and a significant amount of cruelty and ruthlessness our culture is exceedingly uncomfortable with females displaying. Until that sixth book, Anita is a character who wouldn't be out of place in a souped-up Sam Spade world, with all its undercurrents of cruelty, perversion, weariness (not to mention situational ethics driven by need instead of love), and violence.

Let's not forget the violence. It's important to keep in mind that the critical defining factor of ambiguous Anita is her attitude toward violence—or more specifically, her lack of guilt over applying extreme sanctions to "monsters."

But let's not get ahead of ourselves, dear reader.

When discussing Anita and "strong female characters," Joss Whedon's *Buffy the Vampire Slayer* often comes up. There is a critical difference between Buffy and Anita, and it's not just the age divide. Buffy Summers, for all her strength, power, and snappy dialogue, is basically a *passive recipient* of a talent that forces her to fight darkness. The Buffy cycle derives most of its narrative drive from constantly exploiting the tension between those powers and Buffy's oft-expressed and central desire to be a "normal" teenager instead of a reluctant freak. While this may be an excellent vehicle for exploring female teen sexuality and the frightening charge of sex and foreign adult responsibility every young girl faces in the process of maturing, Buffy is still essentially passive, and eternally on the cusp of adulthood.

Anita, however, is introduced to us as a full-fledged adult, however emotionally stunted. She is an *active recipient* of her powers, trained in their use from childhood by her grandmother and displaying surprisingly little angst over them. In fact, Anita's powers are how she earns her adult living. They place her in the role of judge, jury, and executioner; whereas Buffy is no more, when all is said and done, than a supernatural cockroach exterminator.

If Buffy is struggling to move from the black-and-white world of teenage certainty into the gray shadows of adult consequences, Anita has crossed that border and (for the first five to six books, at least) is at home in the shifting sands and ethical quagmires of adulthood.

Buffy has a clear-cut mission—rid the world of Evil. You bet. But Anita is caught weighing the cost of each action, asking which evil is the one that really needs to be eliminated. This is a question our culture is exceedingly uncomfortable with a woman solving openly and physically, despite the fact that adult women (just like adult men) weigh relative and shifting factors of risk, consequence, and responsibility as a matter of course.

We're just not used to seeing a woman weigh those factors with a Browning Hi-Power.

While Anita's gender does not make her special per se, the combination of her gender and the moral and ethical ambiguity of her character, especially when it comes to the use of violence, makes her groundbreaking in the first four books of the series. All strides in feminism aside, girls are *still* supposed to be soft, feminine, nurturing, passive recipients of male action. Films, books, television, ads, magazines—the stew of visual and auditory media we're simmering in holds the assumption of female passivity to be self-evident and therefore a foundation to build our whole worldview on. Women are steeped in unconscious cultural expectations from the cradle—it's rude to run and yell, even if we're running from a rapist/murderer/stalker/etc. I can't count how many times I've heard a female victim of crime say, "I knew something was wrong . . . but I didn't want to be *rude*."

Anita aims her Browning right into the heart of that dynamic and keeps firing and reloading. *She* decides who lives and who dies, and she doesn't give a fig for being rude when her survival is on the line. In the first four books, a constant theme is Anita's extralegal status— she chooses which vampires/monsters die, and (here's the important bit) she feels far less horror and guilt over it than society tells women they *ought* to feel. She feels guilt over her lack of guilt, yes, but instead of seeming shallow, those protestations add complexity to her personality.

Go ahead, Anita says. *Turn around, draw your gun, and kick that monster's ever-loving ass. Kill him before he kills you.*

Strong stuff. *Heady* stuff. Especially in a society where women are taught from birth not to be "rude"—even when the monster is breathing down their necks.

Anita's relationships with males are all marked by this ambiguity. There is Dolph, the standard "abrasive buddy," whose main purpose seems to be highlighting that Anita is an anomaly. Dolph's tamped-down professional appearance shouts that he is the image of the Good Man whose proper place it is to be the active part in their partnership, and his friction with Anita comes when Anita is either most "active" in deciding who lives and dies—or when Anita betrays her stated purpose of policing the monsters and starts considering sleeping with them.

The double standard, apparently, is alive and well, even when a girl is engaging in homicide rather than premarital nookie.

A more problematic relationship is Anita's interaction with Richard the werewolf. Unfortunately, the point at which Anita starts dating him is when a large bit of Anita's fascinating ambiguity and tension begins draining away, like *Moonlighting* after Bruce Willis and Cybil Shepherd's characters started bumping uglies. The chemistry and tension that had sustained their relationship vanished, and so did the show's quality. Once Anita starts on the slippery slope of *dating* monsters instead of *killing* them, large chunks of her psychological complexity are struck off the map.

However, the main problem with Anita and Richard isn't even their relationship—it's Richard's inability to deal with Anita's moral and ethical flexibility. If Dolph is the Good Man, Richard is that Freudian monster the Emasculated Boyfriend, the male fear that strong females will somehow detract from their (apparently finite) stores of masculinity.

This could have added complexity instead of detracting it. As one fellow Anita reader so memorably put it to me, "Richard turns into a whiny passive-aggressive little bitch." Which neatly encapsulates several issues—the pejorative nature of the term "bitch," for one, and the male response to ambiguous and powerful females, for another.

But then there's Jean-Claude.

Balanced against Richard's emasculation is the über-perfect Jean-Claude and his relationship with Anita, in some ways the most treacherous of the lot. Jean-Claude is supernally beautiful, powerful, and sexual, a dark creature (in the first four to six novels) of ambiguity to match Anita's own. It is a marriage made in Hell, however, because once Anita views him as a potential mate and not simply as a sexually threatening monster who doesn't deserve murder *yet*, more of the narrative drive created by Anita's vaunted ambiguity flies straight out the window.

The heart of this problem lies in the territory of sex. As long as there was merely the promise of sex between Anita and Jean-Claude, the uncertainty of their exact relationship—and the level of sexual threat to Anita's psyche—could be exploited for maximum narrative tension. Once Jean-Claude becomes the paradigm of the perfect partner (sexual but nonthreatening in a procreative way, "dangerous" but not to the heroine), he becomes the Good Bad Boy instead of the Demon Lover, and the noir-erotic element of the Blake novels is passed over for the element of personal relationships, also known as the romance genre.

The romance genre is big business, fiction written by women for women. There are stringent conventions and expectations within the genre, from the happy ending to the dance of attraction. Romance both mirrors and subverts conversations about gender roles and expectations, but it does so using an overarching, slow-changing social narrative. The sources of dramatic tension are necessarily different; crossover between romance and noir is problematic because the two genres have wildly divergent aims, and because noir is necessarily *outside* the overarching social narrative the romance genre is working within. (One is not intrinsically more worthy or serious than the other, but they are different phyla, not to mention genus and species.) Even a writer who uses significant noir elements, like Anne Stuart, confines those elements to the male heroes and uses them in the context of that social narrative.

Anita Blake did not start out inside the romance narrative. The walloping of gender expectations fueled by our uncertainty over whether Anita is going to fuck Jean-Claude or kill him (a dynamic played out between every shifty dame and hardboiled gumshoe in damn near every noir tale) has muted in recent books into the playing-out of more socially conventional gender roles—whether or not Jean-Claude and Anita can *communicate* enough to "fix" their relationship. Likewise, our uncertainty over Jean-Claude's behavior—whether or not *he's* going to kill Anita or fuck her, once she lets her guard down—has moved out of the realm of ambiguity and into the realm of boyfriend-girlfriend.

All the gunpowder and scary volatility of Anita and Jean-Claude, all that trainwreck factor you just can't look away from, vanishes.

And what about Edward? Relax, we'll get to him in a minute.

Anita's relationship with female figures is secondary to her relationship with males. The females in Anita Blake's world are either standpoints of conventionality, serving as a Greek chorus to highlight social gender expectations (like Ronnie), or they are embodiments of the Dark Feminine without Anita's redeeming qualities (for example, Nikolaos). Of all of these, two deserve particular attention: Ronnie and Raina.

While Anita is still ambiguous, Ronnie can be seen as Anita's foot in the world of conventional gender expectations. Despite the hay made of Ronnie's sexual behavior in the first books of the series, she is still a character we can find unthreatening. She completely lacks Anita's edge of raw violent power, since she isn't claiming the right of murder. Ronnie does not decide who lives or dies, so her sexual peccadilloes are not nearly as fascinating or threatening as Anita's. Ronnie could be Anita's alter ego, the "safe" woman Anita could have been if not for her talents and active pursuit of violence to even the scales.

In other words, it's okay for Ronnie to be *Sex in the City,* as long as she's not packing heat or prepared to use it without guilt. One wonders if this contrast was drawn consciously by Hamilton, or if it was merely a Janus-faced happy accident.

In the beginning of the series, Anita has to a large extent chosen her career over sex, and Ronnie is conventionally (and actively)

sexual in a way Anita cannot be if she hopes to remain a noir character. As long as Anita stayed in the territory of murderous ambiguity,
which also meant remaining largely sexually uninterested, the friendship survived, as friendships of individuals with different but roughly
equal social niches often do, with each partner bringing something
to the table.

However, once Anita's focus moved from noir ambiguity to personal relationships, Ronnie's status as the voice of conventional gender interaction was compromised. The character's response to this is
twofold: Ronnie must become even more conventional (i.e., monogamous) to survive in the series and serve a purpose; and the element
of jealousy and "traditional" feminine backstabbing is introduced to
take the place of the early tension between Anita's ethical gray areas
and Ronnie's espousal of more conventional values.

In other words, once Anita becomes sexually active in an "acceptable" or "normal" way—once her focus becomes the relationships with men in her life, even if there are rather a lot of them—she
becomes not a friend to Ronnie but a rival, and their relationship
takes on the tone of a formerly popular cheerleader versus the cheerleader who's popular now.

The reader almost wishes for a dose of *Heathers*-esque rat poison
to sort the two out.

The sadistic lycanthrope Raina suffers as well. As an embodiment of the destructive Dark Feminine, Raina is perhaps without
equal in the Blake series, and her refusal to be a decent sport and go
away when killed is one of the true flashes of subconscious genius
on Hamilton's part. Raina is unapologetically and unashamedly the
castrating, child-eating female Freudians crawl under their beds in
fear of. She is a twilit, liminal figure, built to show just how Anita as
the protagonist is balanced on the threshold between light ("good,"
conventional morality) and dark (Raina herself). *Look*, Raina says, *you
could end up like me. What stops you from ending up like me?*

And Anita's response, while at her tight best in the first four to six
novels, is a chilling challenge: *What makes you think I won't?*

Unfortunately, the moral and ethical ambiguity of noir depends
on that balancing act. The further a protagonist moves toward the

light of convention, the more the dark recedes. The teeter-totter thumps down on one side, all tension keeping the two characters balanced is lost, and Raina, stranded in midair, becomes not a figure of terror but a postscript.

In any case, Anita's primary relationships all through the series are with men. At first she defines herself in opposition to both male expectations and acceptable female behavior in the face of those expectations, which adds the delicious *frisson* of feminism's attempts to create female roles that are not defined by feminine utility as viewed by males. The instant Anita steps out of the exploration of ethics, morality, and violence and into the exploration of personal relationships tainted with conventional gender roles, she becomes not an *ambiguous* female character but a *merely* female one. She loses a large chunk of the mysterious tension that makes her such a compelling protagonist.

Which leads us to Edward.

Edward, as Anita's fellow killer and pioneer at the frontier of ethical ambiguity, serves as the male half of the noir exploration in earlier Blake books. Even Anita isn't sure whether or not he's going to kill her once he decides he should, and one can only presume Edward returns the favor.

We have two halves of a perfectly balanced coin here; the Vampire Executioner series could have just as easily been about Edward. The fact that Anita is female makes her moral and ethical transgressions so much more compelling. When all is said and done, society is far more comfortable with aggressive, morally flexible male killers than with females who share the same qualities. Just look at all the Clive Cussler, Tom Clancy, *Executioner,* and male superhero-based comic books out there. Violence is traditionally the purview of the male.

After all, girls don't want to be "rude."

Edward's function is to underscore Anita's difference. She is a girl who can play with the boys as an equal, on her own terms. The two have found a commonality of violence, and Edward's attempts to make Anita an honorary "man" were met in earlier books by Anita's stubborn refusal to step out of the gray ethical area engendered (ha ha) by her gender. We presume Edward never thinks too much about the monsters he kills; he is perilously close to being, like Buffy, merely an Extermination of Supernatural Insects Specialist. What makes Anita the protagonist, and a wonderfully compelling protagonist at that, is the balance between her capacity for cold-blooded murder in service to the law and the mulling over of the ethical and moral issues and quandaries raised by cold-blooded murder in service to the law.

Testosterone-driven stories of male lawgivers separated from lawbreakers only by a freak of ethical circumstance are everywhere. We have a positive hunger in our society for stories about cops or decorated military men going on rampages of violence that are acceptable for various "moral" reasons. (Rambo. The Punisher. Lorenzo Carcaterra's *Apaches* and *Sleepers*, Dennis Lehane's *Mystic River*, the terrorfest of *24* . . . need I go on? And let's not even *talk* about the Western genre. . . .) By switching the gender of the protagonist, a fresh wellspring of transgressive tension is suddenly created and gleefully plundered.

In some senses, Anita's only true relationship consistently untainted by traditional gender roles is with Edward. He could care less what dangly bits she has. He only cares if she's able and willing to back him against the monsters. Descriptions of Edward and Anita's interactions are fueled by a breathless tension far more incredibly sexual in its intensity than any seduction scene between Anita and Jean-Claude. Jean-Claude, merely by engaging in sex with Anita, becomes a victim of traditional roles and fits neatly into a predetermined slot. Edward, however, still retains the charge of the transgressive, the ambiguous, the violent, the mysterious holder of the power of life and death.

The more Anita moves toward a focus on personal relationships, the more Edward recedes like Raina. The fringe ceases to become visible the closer one moves to the mainstream. And all of Edward's highly charged power as the mirror (male) image of Anita drains away once Anita does not mirror him. Once again, one end of the teeter-totter thumps down to earth, and one-half of the equation is left high and dry while the other half is marooned in dusty clay. Edward, the husband and dad with a "secret," is a recognizable figure (like any

CIA or FBI man in male-driven genre fiction) instead of a transgressive, liminal one.

Again, this is not to say that a focus on personal relationships is a bad thing. Both the genres that focus on the theme of personal relationships—a subsection of lit fic and the romance genre—have their own sources of dramatic tension and their own ways of examining gender roles and mores as well as the transgressing of the same.

The romance genre, in particular, has served as an ongoing conversation about femininity and gender roles. The gothics and Victoria Holt virgins of the seventies led to the boardroom virgins and sheikh kidnappings of the eighties, which gave way to the slightly more diversified (but still prone to a good forced-seduction) nineties, all leading to the chick-lit and paranormals of the naughts. We can only guess at what new forms the conversation will take in the future. The romance field is a behemoth and a shapeshifter, much like the fantasy field itself, where Anita first made her home.

What made Anita unique to me was her moral and ethical ambiguity as a female protagonist. In Anita's footsteps have followed a slew of kickass urban-fantasy heroines, with varying degrees of ambiguity when it comes to murder and mayhem. Very few of them approach the level of tension in the first four Blake books; the superlative among them seem to rest in a comfortable hinterland at the level of, say, *Burnt Offerings*, the last book where I was genuinely uncertain whether Anita and Jean-Claude were going to kill each other—or fall into bed. The rest tend to clump in a group that either fall more neatly into the romance genre (the exploration of personal relationships) or deal with ethical ambiguity at about a quarter of the intensity of the first Blake novels.

Anita's ambiguity rested for me on her uncompromising, fierce adherence to her own ethical code *and* her refusal to overly flagellate herself with guilt over the "murder" of monsters. At its best, this dynamic approached a feverish, nightmarish, *Silence of the Lambs* intensity. At its most chilling, it led the reader to examine just how uncomfortable the thought of a woman with a gun and a reason to use it makes anyone raised with our cultural gender expectations.

To me, the shift toward personal relationships in the Anita Blake series robs the characters, both primary and secondary, of a great deal of tension and immediacy. And yet, the early Blake novels kicked in the door of fantasy with a Browning Hi-Power in either hand, eyes narrowed and alight with hellish fire. The idea of a female protagonist who feels little guilt over the murder she does for society was a gigantic kick in the literary balls, so to speak, and a whole generation of urban fantasy writers owe a huge debt of gratitude to Anita Blake for that particular nut-shot.

Early Anita Blake was a direct descendant of those gumshoes in Raymond Chandler or Dashiell Hammett shorts and novels. The scarred, fictional men who moved in perpetual twilight, physically as well as ethically, trying to be decent in a not-so-decent world, can be proud of their daughter Anita for breaking new ground. If she has moved out of that twilight, it is nobody's business but hers—but still, I long sometimes for a return to the good old bad days of Anita, where the monsters were monsters, not Stepford lycanthropes, and the only way to meet them was with the understanding that you might be killing them tomorrow no matter how useful—or sexually charged—they are today.

But then, I always wanted the noir gumshoe to go off into the sunset with his smartmouth secretary instead of mooning over the heartless dame who would give him trouble, too. The problem with ambiguous characters is that they make the reader yearn for an end to the tension, and when that end comes, the reader longs for the old breathless excitement of not knowing which way the protagonist—and, therefore, the reader herself—is going to jump.

As Anita herself might say, there's just no pleasing some people, is there.

◆   ◆   ◆

Lilith Saintcrow is the author of several urban fantasy, paranormal romance, and young adult books. She lives in Vancouver, Washington, with her two children, three cats, and assorted other strays.

If you asked me what I write I would say Paranormal Thrillers. It encompasses everything I do, and doesn't try and pigeonhole me. The essay that follows says that I write romances—paranormal romances, but romances—and then proceeds to explain why I've broken all the romance rules. I broke them because no one told me there were any rules, because I hadn't read a "romance" since junior high and that was a Harlequin back in the day when they were all squeaky clean and the barest hint of sex was all you had. Love conquers all: I knew that was a lie by the time I was ten. The adults around me had proven that. In fact, when I was young I was never getting married. I never dreamed of my wedding, or fantasized about the perfect man, because I didn't believe in a perfect anything. By the time I was teenager I'd seen too much harsh reality, real violence, death. It's not the stuff to make you daydream about Prince Charming. By age fourteen or fifteen I knew that if anyone was going to save my ass, it was going to have to be me. A lot of my girlfriends read romances, but I just didn't understand the idea of them. The premise escaped me. So imagine my surprise when I started writing what I thought was a horror/mystery series about Anita Blake who raised the dead and executed vampires for the government, and was told it was a romance series. Romance? Me? Surely not.

When *Buffy the Vampire Slayer* came on TV I'd been writing this stuff for years, but she had her Angel and I could see that it was romantic. I could see that Jean-Claude and Anita was romantic, and that Anita and Richard was romantic, but I still thought of the books as a mystery series—one with vampires and werewolves, but still a mystery series. But a lot of my female audience thought of them as romances. That was fine with me, until I wrote the unforgiveable. I had Anita choose the wrong man.

Oh, dear God, I took crap for her sleeping with the vampire and not the good little werewolf. Then later on I took even more crap because having slept with both she chose to leave both their asses and try to maintain her own identity. And then, I apparently committed the last and most unforgiveable romance crime, I brought in a new man out of the blue, Micah, and had her fall for him. I have never had such hatred directed toward me as I did when *Narcissus in Chains* came out. Richard, our good little werewolf, had dumped Anita, but the fans were so adamant that she had dumped him I actually went back and reread the scene, thinking I was misremembering. But no, he dumps her. But somehow it was her fault, my fault. It was as if I'd personally dumped their favorite brother.

I didn't understand it then, and really don't now, but this essay explains by not even mentioning the other men. The essay talks about romance and talks only about Richard and Jean-Claude, the up-right good guy and the seductive bad boy, werewolf and vampire respectively. The other men are only hinted at, and that sums up the reason I am not romance. I've broken too many rules. I'm not mystery because I've broken their genre rules by having the relationships be important. I am neither fish nor fowl, for any genre. Let me say that my female readership has continued to grow since I broke these rules, and my male readership has grown by leaps and bounds, too. Sometimes by not fitting in you find that you're not the only one who felt restricted by the rules. I write Paranormal Thrillers, and for that definition, if you need one, I fit just fine.

◆

◆

◆

—Laurell

Dating the Monsters

Why It Takes
a Vampire or a Wereguy
to Win the Heart of the Modern It Girl

L. JAGI LAMPLIGHTER

T ime was when the Romance section of the bookstore was a safe and cozy retreat from all things unfrivolous. Sure, there might be an occasional gothic or mystery romance with a terrifying moment or two, but one could basically rely on the fact that any book you took off the shelves would be like eating spun sugar. Going to buy a romance novel was like visiting the confectionary section of a bakery.

Not anymore! Where once dwelt only roses and Almack's, now live vampires, demons, werewolves, Greek gods, and yes, even robots. Though, most of all, it is vampires. And not all these books are sugar sweet, either. It's like heading down to the confectionary and finding yourself in hot spicy foods instead!

By now, you are probably asking yourself: How did this happen, and what does it have to do with Anita Blake?

Buffy, Anita Blake, and the Paranormal Romance Invasion

It started on television with *Buffy the Vampire Slayer*, but it was Laurell K. Hamilton and Anita Blake who brought stories of girls and monsters to the world of popular books. Though paranormal romance is now a booming business, Anita Blake still leads the way, a giant striding amongst her younger sisters. Anita both kills the monsters and dates them. It's like having your cake and shooting it, too.

The question naturally arises: Why monsters? What is it about vampires and werewolves—once only the stuff of horror stories—that makes them the ideal modern romantic hero? To find the answer, we must first examine the age-old war between culture and drama.

The Needs of Culture Vs. the Needs of Drama

Throughout history, a tug of war has existed between the desire to use stories to teach and the desire for them to entertain. At times, such as the Middle Ages with its passion plays, teaching has won out completely. Other times, such as Shakespeare's age, entertainment triumphed. (It is amusing to look back and recall that Shakespeare's plays, which so many children dread reading in English class today, were written as pure entertainment for the masses!)

The desire to use stories to teach, I shall call for the purpose of this essay "the needs of culture." Proponents of this idea hope to use the medium of entertainment to lead people to make the choices necessary for a moral, law abiding society. Such societies are great to live in—not fearing that you are going to be carjacked or molested really makes a person's day. And if we could make our children truthful, upright, and brave through examples in literature, that would be a very gratifying indeed!

The problem is that, most of the time, the more pleasant a culture is to live in, the less interesting it is to read about. A really fine writer can make anything interesting, but few writers achieve this pinnacle of brilliance. It takes a superb writer to make the process of painting a landscape interesting to an outsider. It only takes a writer of ordinary skill to bring excitement to a chase scene with a thief and a company assassin on ski mobiles in the midst of the Winter Olympics.

In our entertainment today, the needs of drama often outweigh the needs of culture. We would like to teach our children to be peaceful and chaste, but violence and sex sell. They draw readers.

But this does not keep the guardians of culture from criticizing our entertainment when it falls short of the demands of culture.

So What Are the Needs of Culture?

What are the values those who favor improving the culture wish to put across? Currently, they fall into two categories: traditional cultural values and modern cultural values.

Traditional culture covers the kind of thing listed in the Ten Commandments or the Boy Scouts' pledge. It wants people to be honest, upright, brave, clean, etc. The needs of traditional culture require that good guys be upright, bad guys always get their comeuppance, and the line between the two remains crisply defined.

Modern culture, too, has needs, things it wants drama to portray as good and to encourage in its audience. This desire is so prevalent in our society that it has its own name: political correctness. Races must get along. All people, regardless of rank or birth, must be treated as equals. The old taboos are to be laid to rest; no one needs them anymore. Nobility and grandeur are to be sneered at, and women must be the equal of men.

What About the Needs of Drama?

The needs of drama are quite different from those of culture. They are ruled by the desire to entertain. Whatever enthralls the audience most, that is what drama requires. Unfortunately for those who would use stories to teach cultural mores, what makes a story entertaining is often directly at odds with what is good or virtuous or politically correct.

Drama is about conflict. It is about breaking taboos, the more shocking the better! Thieves, prostitutes, gamblers, alcoholics, adulterers—all the things that traditional culture does not wish to glamorize—make for entrancing drama. But it is not just traditional culture that gets trampled by the needs of drama. Bigotry, class struggles, and inequality among the sexes also make for excellent storytelling.

Are the people who fear the effect of drama on society starting at shadows? Perhaps not. Shock value is temporary. The moment you have seen a few stories that violate a particular taboo, that tension becomes old hat. Nobody cares anymore. There is no sense of surprise. People do not care if they see the same thing in another movie. They start thinking of that particular behavior as normal, or at least as a part of reality that must be endured.

So those who wish they could guard culture by controlling drama do have a strong argument on their side. But they cannot change the facts: a story that explores boundaries and breaks taboos is often a better story than one that does not.

Of course, these categories are only generalizations. The same story can serve both forces at different times or support some cultural values while chipping away at others. For the sake of simplicity, however, they will be discussed here as if they are distinct categories.

Love's Savage Fury

When I was younger, I was too embarrassed to admit that I read romances. I used to hide them under other books or read them only when I was entirely alone. After all, women were the equals of men; that meant we should act like men in all ways, right? Indulging in any feminine behavior was frowned upon, and what was more feminine than reading about Vikings carrying off swooning maidens? No modern woman would allow herself to be treated in such a fashion! So why would she encourage the degradation of her sisters by buying books that glorified such behavior?

As I got older—and learned that a higher percentage of romances are sold each year than any other type of book—I decided I should not be ashamed. I should stand up for what I enjoyed—even if it was curling up by the fire and letting myself be swept away by the trials of love. So I came out of the romance closet (which is pink inside and hung with lace and portraits of Fabio. That alone was motivation to get me out of there. Never really been a Fabio fan. Had I had my way, I would have decorated the place with posters of Adrian Paul.).

But what is romance? What makes a romance reader sigh and snuggle down among the pillows on her love seat or sit hugging a box of tissues as she reads, tears running down her cheeks? Or, more to the point, what is a reader looking for when she stops by for a taste of spun sugar or even hot spice?

First and foremost, she is looking to be swept away, to feel that wonderful tingle of feminine emotion as Rhett carries Scarlett up the stairs, as Elizabeth realizes that she loves Darcy, as Buffy falls for Angel, as Anita finally chooses between Richard and Jean-Claude. There is a reason that romances have titles such as *Savage Passion* and *Love's Savage Fury*. That heady tingly-girly feeling that sweeps away the reader requires two things: obstacles that give the couple time to build up sexual tension before being brought together and an exaggeration of the masculine and feminine qualities—the dominant and authoritative vs. the graceful and nurturing.

Or in other words, taboos and inequality between the sexes.

Taboo or Not Taboo

Of all genres, none relies upon taboos as heavily as romance. The romance—a.k.a. the story of girl meets boy, boy chases girl, girl gets boy—requires obstacles to keep our heroine from snagging her man right away. Taboos—cultural reasons why the two should not be together—are among the most compelling.

Commoners cannot marry noblemen. Montagues are forbidden to marry Capulets. Good devout children are forbidden to marry outside their religion, whether they are Catholic, Protestant, Jew, or Hindu. Harem girls cannot fall in love—with anyone! Some of the best romances, and the best novels altogether, are about lovers who cross these boundaries, whose love bridges the taboo gap.

It is here, in the land of taboos, that the needs of modern culture and the needs of romance clash most drastically.

Modern culture does not like old-fashioned taboos. It frowns upon them and removes them from society. The old taboos that kept men and women apart are a thing of the past. Nowadays, nothing except inclination stops partners from jumping directly into bed the first instance they meet.

Socially, there is much to praise about this lack of false obstacles; however, free access to the opposite sex is the death knell of romance—

or at least of romantic drama. This is one reason that historical romances are so popular. Romances set in times when taboos governed how men and women could interact, when they could see each other, and whether they could snatch a few moments alone come automatically primed with all the necessary ingredients for tension and conflict.

All Is Fair in Love and War

So, what exactly causes this tingly-girly feeling? What creates a sense of romance? Romance comes from the struggle of two lovers to come together—but not just any struggle with any outcome. There is a set of principles by which the romance world operates. They are the three unspoken promises that draw the story along.

The first is: *love conquers all*. It does not matter what promises are broken or what sins are committed because the reader knows in her heart that love will set everything aright in the end. The very laws of the universe will rearrange fate to reunite the lovers. Their missteps will turn out to be justified, and all crimes will be excused when love triumphs over all.

The second is: *true love pierces all illusions*. No matter how wild or unkempt the man, no matter how dowdy the girl, the reader knows that their true love, the one person for whom they are meant, will pierce this false veil and see their true self shining beneath. The heroine can spot the prince where the rest of the world sees only a monster. The hero can see the pearl of great price for which he will, if need be, sell all that he has, where eyes not made perfect by love see merely another pretty face.

The third unspoken promise is: *happily ever after*. No matter how dire events may seem, we know that, within the pages of these books, all our hopes will come true. By the last page, we will have won our way to the world of happy marriages, where everyone is filled with joy and has bundles and bundles of children.

Fundamentally, romance is about hope.

No Sissy Men Need Apply

The art of writing a good romance is the art of creating in your reader a rush of the most feminine emotions, the ones that make us weep, catch our breath, and clasp our hands with joy. To do this, the story needs to present a feminine character confronting stark masculinity. Merely the ordinary man, the nice man, is not enough. The romantic hero must have exaggerated masculine qualities so as to create the illusion that he is a cut above those around him in some specific and distinctly masculine way.

Arrogance, violence, brusqueness, bull-headedness—all the qualities modern culture abhors—are the qualities that give the impression of masculinity in a story. Why? Because these qualities seem so alien to most women. The very fact that the hero's behavior is in contrast with the feminine and the ordinary emphasizes his masculinity—so long as he also has definite recognizable virtues to balance them out. The more uncivilized and masculine the hero, the more successful the romance—look at the wild, unruly Rhett Butler as opposed to the gentle, mannerly Ashley Wilkes. Scarlett might love Ashley, but Rhett is the one who captures the reader's heart! The more the man does not do what society expects, the more he exhibits unbridled masculinity, the sexier he seems on paper.

In romances, this boils down to the two archetypical romantic hero types: the playboy and the recluse. The first, the Rhett Butler type—or maybe we should call it the Jean-Claude type—has had so many women that he is immune to being affected by any particular one, until the right girl comes along and catches his heart. The second, the Darcy type, is immune to feminine appeal all together, living a thoroughly masculine, bachelor existence, until the heroine arrives and shatters his stately world.

Because the premise of all romance is, of course, that beauty tames the beast—that *this* woman, the one *right* woman, can rein in those very qualities that make the hero more of a man than those around him. The more exaggerated the hero's unsociable masculine qualities in the beginning of the story, the more of a victory achieved by the heroine.

Of Lords and Pirate Captains

If going all tingly-girly requires manly heroes, how does romance achieve this manliness? An easy way is to make him literally more powerful than the heroine. Remember, romance is about the drama of romantic love, not a paean to the modern idea of equality among the sexes. Oh, the heroine can be spunky! She can take no gruff from no man. But romance works best if she is the social inferior of the hero, when she is at a disadvantage.

This social inferiority allows her pursuer to put pressure on her, to insist that she yield to his demands, and all those yummy things that make romances romantic. It also makes her final victory all the more noteworthy. If a powerful princess wins the heart of a noble-man, no one is surprised. If the younger daughter of an overlooked squire rises from obscurity to transform the hero and win herself a duchy, her accomplishment is far more triumphant.

In historical romances, it is easy to put the hero in a position of power compared to the girl. Historical romance heroes are nearly al-ways lords, highwaymen (who are usually lords in disguise), pirates (who are sometimes lords in disguise), cowboys, Vikings, or Indian braves (*Indian* braves, mind you—which illustrates another clash between the needs of modern culture and the needs of drama. No young woman is filled with feminine thrills at the thought of a being carried off by a Native American. But an Indian!).

Even in present day romances, the men are often lawyers, doc-tors, and businessmen who own the lien on Pa's farm, or cowboys, artists, and gamblers—all professions that are thought to be either powerful or cool. However, contemporary romances seldom have the sparkle of their historical cousins. In our modern culture, men and women are basically equal, and there are very few taboos keeping them apart. When it comes to modern day, it is a dry desert out there for romance writers!

Behold the Super Girl!

Not all stories that serve the purpose of culture are bad. One of the tenets of our modern world is that women can excel at everything, and this concept can be great fun. What modern woman has not wished she had the power to kick butt like Buffy the Vampire Slayer or fly like Supergirl? Who has not wished to see a female character who overthrows the inequalities of the earlier ages?

As a child, I scoured the books available but could find few examples of competent women with spunk—female characters who had it together, got stuff done, and were not intimidated by life. Lessa of Pern stands out as the single exception. Apparently, I was not alone in this desire, because today's audiences have welcomed this golden age of butt-kicking heroines with great relish.

Anita Blake is exactly the kind of character I wished to read about when I was in high school. Particularly Anita as she appeared in the early books, when she was chaste and concerned with her integrity. I loved this! So few characters have integrity these days or refuse to sleep around. It was tremendously refreshing. However, like many modern women, Anita was a character who seemed too large—in the "larger than life" sense—for the men of her age. The ordinary humans she worked with were too weak, too slow to keep up with her.

And here finally, we have the fundamental conflict between modern culture and drama. Culture demanded a heroine who is fierce, powerful, and spunky, who lives in a world without taboos where she can do exactly as she pleases. But the needs of drama, the laws that govern what makes a story romantic, require something else entirely: a superior male who lives in a world where taboos separate the heroine from the object of her desire.

Enter the Monster

Enter the paranormal man. He is dark. He is powerful. He is sexy. And he has taboos galore! He is so powerful, he could kill you with a kiss—if he does not hold himself back. As to taboos . . . well, he is supernatural. This opens the way for the author to invent as many taboos as she pleases: he cannot face the sunlight, cannot come out on the full moon, cannot talk to mortals, cannot this, cannot that, and cannot the other!

A paranormal man, a creature with supernatural powers, is automatically the social superior of any ordinary human in the mind of the reader. True, vampires and werewolves are often outcasts in society, but the moment a superhuman is introduced in a story, fans begin to lose interest in the mundane. They want to find out what is going on in the elite supernatural community.

By turning the romantic hero into a supernatural being, one can have both the glories of a competent powerful heroine, and the taboos and inequalities necessary for a satisfying romance.

When paranormal romances first hit the bookshelves, they came in all flavors: Greek gods and robots wooed their maidens beside their darker counterparts. Now, only a few years later, the darker counterparts, the vampire and the werewolf, have proven to be the breakout stars. Every third book in the romance stacks seems to have blood dripping on its roses.

But why are monsters—vampires, werewolves, demons, and the like—so much more popular as romantic heroes than gods, fairies, and—okay, I can see why robots did not really take off—other less horrific creatures?

Because violence is masculine. The more violent the hero, and the more he is ravaged by desires he cannot control—the desire for blood, the uncontrollable compulsion to turn into a wolf under the full moon—the more excuse for the hero to allow his passions to run away with him, and the greater the heroine's victory when she ultimately tames him!

Anita in Love

Which brings us back to Anita Blake and her many monster loves.

Nearly everyone I know who reads paranormal romances started with Anita Blake. Some of them read the early Anita books and now look elsewhere for stories that are more squarely in the romance genre. Others still enjoy Anita, but have also branched out, looking for similar types of titles in the romance and fantasy sections of their local bookstore.

In the early Anita books, the romance sizzles! All the elements are present for the ultimate feminine thrill: A chaste heroine. A powerful yet sensuous Master of men and monsters who will stop at nothing to get the girl. A gentler, more thoughtful man who has all the qualities a girl should desire and yet lacks the fascination and edge of the first man. And keeping them apart? Taboos galore!

Jean-Claude cannot come out during the day. He cannot be seen as weak in front of his people. Richard cannot let the general community know he is a werewolf if he wishes to keep his teaching job. Meanwhile, the other wolves want to force him to live up to their codes, which include yet more restrictions on how he should act and comport himself.

It's ideal! Romantic heaven!

A brief word on the difference between the early and later Anita books: One important aspect of traditional romance is the illusion that the heroine has a true love, that she is planning to pick one of her suitors and give the rest of them the boot. Once the character relinquishes this goal and entertains the notion of keeping many men around on a permanent basis, the story becomes something other than a romance. (I'm not sure what that is, but the Japanese have a genre for stories where a guy lives with a huge group of pretty women whom he cannot seem to choose between. They call them "harem anime.")

The Hero of Culture Vs. the Hero of Drama

The moment when Anita finally chooses one of the two suitors who have been wooing her for a number of books is one of the most satisfying scenes in romancedom. We readers had waited so long! Whether the guy Anita chose was the one we preferred or not, having her make her choice was like leaping into a cold, crashing wave after running along the beach for a long time on a very hot day.

And yet, the question arises, did Anita make the right choice? Could she have chosen the other man? And how do the needs of culture and drama figure into her decision?

Jean-Claude is a perfect example of the dramatic romantic hero. He is the Master of the City, with all manner of minions at his beck and call, deadly as sin, and so sexy that grown women lean languidly against walls and sigh whenever his name is mentioned. (My husband can vouch for having seen the mere mention of Jean-Claude have this effect on any number of women.)

Jean-Claude is the ultimate playboy. He glides through life with his shirt open, surrounded by an aura of sensuality, using everything around him for his own pleasure and being touched by nothing. His status is increased by the fact that he is desired by everything that moves: men, women, dogs (well, wolves). Tricycles would lust after Jean-Claude if they could move of their own accord. And he is monstrous. He is callous. He kills. He drinks blood. He does not obey the dictates of society nor care for the opinions of others.

Nor is he thoroughly immoral—for that would not be romantic. He has his own code he struggles to live up to, related to his position and his responsibility to the people under his protection. This tension between his wickedness and his decent streak makes him all the more appealing.

Richard is a different kind of hero. He epitomizes modern culture's notion of the ideal man: good-looking, understanding, a good listener. But of course Richard isn't without an edge, and that's part of his appeal. He turns into a wolf once a month and pushes other wolf-boys around. That, and the fact that the local wolf pack thinks he belongs to them, creates all kinds of havoc with his dating life.

What more could a girl desire?

Face it, if Anita were our girlfriend in real life, we all know which guy we would be rooting for—the kind, thoughtful, easy-going man who loves children! He is every parent's dream—well, except for the werewolf thing, but we can see past that. He is the kind of man you want your friend to marry. Someone who will make her happy, and in Anita's case, keep her human. Sure, he loses it when the moon is full, but hey, in a few years he'll be able to take something for that, and his furry problem will be a thing of the past.

But Anita does not live in the real world. She lives in the realm of entertainment, and there, the laws of drama rule. The choice that serves the needs of drama is the one that pushes the envelope, that drives the heroine beyond her comfort zone, that requires more of her—mind, body, and soul—if she is to survive and if love is to triumph. So, with apologies to my dear friend who thinks that the junior high teacher with the silky chestnut hair is the hottest number out there:

Richard Zeeman never had a chance.

Beauty and The Beast Revisited

Romance is, fundamentally, the story of Beauty and the Beast, told and retold a hundred thousand ways. Beauty's love allows her to see through the Beast's rough exterior and to transform him into the man he is meant to be. In the past, the hero's beast-like qualities manifested in his behavior. Modern heroes are no different; they have just shed their semblance of humanity and now appear as the untamed beasts they really are—sharp fangs, furry backsides, and all. The result, however, is still the same. By the end of the story, love has turned them into a prince, and they live happily ever after.

And Anita Blake? The romantics among her fans are still holding out for a happy ending: that, when all is said and done, love will conquer, and Anita will get her man. True, she may chose to permanently walk another path. Her happy ending may not include just one true love—but hey . . . a girl can hope!

❖   ❖   ❖

L. Jagi Lamplighter is the author of the Prospero's Daughter series, the first book of which, *Prospero Lost*, is available. She is also an assistant editor on the Bad Ass Faeries Anthology series. When not writing, she switches to her secret identity as wife and stay-home mom in Centreville, Virginia, where she lives with her dashing husband, author John C. Wright, and their four darling children, Orville, Roland Wilbur, Justinian Oberon, and Pingping.

She can be found blogging at http://arhyalon.livejournal.com.

Marella is a member of my writing group, so she knows that in the early days of writing the Anita Blake series I was adamant that Anita would never have sex on paper, and she certainly wouldn't have sex with Jean-Claude. I believed what I wrote, that you didn't have sex with dead guys. I mean, a girl's got to have standards. Lack of pulse should take someone off your list.

Jean-Claude tried to take over my series, and by book three, *Circus of the Damned*, I'd decided to kill him off to keep him from doing it. When Anita and I couldn't do the deed I brought on Richard Zeeman, werewolf, junior high science teacher, and good guy, to date and marry Anita. If I couldn't kill the vampire off, I'd take him out of the game with monogamy. From the moment I tried to push Anita to go with Richard I lost control of the series. The harder I pushed the more the characters pushed back and it just didn't work out the way I'd planned.

My plan had been to make every caress, every kiss, so amazing we'd never have to have sex on paper. What I ended up doing was writing myself into a corner. When in book six, *The Killing Dance*, we finally crossed that barrier, I wanted to do that 1940s pan to the sky. I so did not want to show the dirty deed on paper. But for five books I had been unflinching in showing violence on paper. Now, I'd done it because the book plots usually revolved around a murder and that's usually violent. I showed the level of violence that was necessary to tell the story. The fact that the violence hadn't bothered me, but the sex did, made me question my priorities. Sex between two people who cared for each other, and had waited books to have sex, made me squirm. What did that say about me as a person? Well, actually, that I was very American. But the moment I realized it bothered me I had to overcome it. I had to push myself to do the best scene I could do. For Anita, for Jean-Claude, for my readers, for myself, it had to kick major ass.

I don't know if I've ever rewritten a single scene so many times. My friend and artist Paty Cockrun was the person I sent it to for the first reading. She's been a huge Jean-Claude fan through all the books. She always hated Richard. She made me rewrite the scene with Jean-Claude and Anita in the bathtub two more times. But when I sent it to her the next time, she pronounced it good. I have since signed copies of *Killing Dance* on the pages where the sex takes place. Fans have their favorite parts and some even have me sign in between the lines of their favorite moment.

Since that first sex scene I have written a lot more of them. Whatever hesitation or squeamishness I had in the beginning is pretty much gone. I've read the scenes in public, and there's no embarrassment on my end. Sex between consenting adults who care for each other is never a bad thing.

Marella makes one other very good point. The English language sucks on vocabulary for sex. We have no good words. My favorite word for describing a sex act isn't one that normally gets used about heterosexual intercourse. Want to hear it? My favorite word for a sexual act in the English language is: sodomy. There is no word as pretty to describe anything a heterosexual couple would do. (Of course, by some definitions sodomy can happen between heterosexual couples. It's still the same definition, isn't it? Well, yes, I think so.) I have been trying to find a pretty word for heterosexual intercourse for years, but, alas, there is nothing half so lyrical in English.

—*Laurell*

Bon Rapports

MARELLA SANDS

I t's an old and well-used maxim that you gotta start with a joke. With that in mind, I'd like to tell you about the time Ms. Hamilton announced that she would never, ever write a sex scene. It was an ironclad rule: *No Sex On Stage*.

That's right. No sex for Anita. Ever. At least, not in front of her readers.

Stop laughing. I can hear you from here, you know. Honest, she really said that. And with a long tradition of sexy but not sexual vampires in the literature, there was no reason to suspect at the time that Anita would ever be sleeping with the undead, except possibly in a purely literal fashion.

Sure, the phrase *sleep with* to mean sexual intercourse has been servicing the law, and authors, since at least the tenth century. But as late as the nineteenth century, while everyone and his dog were probably humping everything in sight (though, we hope, not each other), no one was going to talk about it. Even though *humping* as an alternative to *sleep with* had evolved by the late 1700s (*servicing* was even older than that) and was clearly available, titillating readers rather than thrusting sex in their faces was the order of the day.

Call it the age of coyness, at least ideally. John Polidori, the first to mingle vampires and noblemen, wrote that his vampire, Lord Ruthven, in the story "The Vampyre: A Tale," seduced women so that they were "hurled from the pinnacle of unsullied virtue, down to the lowest abyss of infamy and degradation." In fact, so sullied were they, that they became wantons who cared nothing for their reputations or those of their families. They "had not scrupled to expose the whole deformity of their vices to the public gaze." One suspects that Polidori, if not familiar with much sexual licentiousness before meeting his employer, Lord Byron, was much more educated afterward, and yet, his prose remained proper. Despite the swath Lord Ruthven cut through the unsullied young women of Europe, the author's eyes remained politely averted while all of this degradation was actually taking place.

Well! Long gone are the days when phrases like "hurled from the pinnacle of unsullied virtue" could make a reader hot and bothered. Anita, of course, has no patience for such long-windedness, and anyone who's managed to get to the end of Polidori's story might be forgiven for wanting to hire Anita to stake him simply for his run-on sentences. (One hopes he was a better doctor than he was a writer.) By concentrating on heiresses hurled from pinnacles rather than depicting characters *putting the sour cream in the burrito*, Polidori had successfully *stormed the pearly gates* with the English of his time. But we've come a long way since then, haven't we?

Literature no longer requires coy phrases like "hurled to the lowest abyss of degradation." And yet, even so, for the modern author, English still sucks donkey balls sometimes. Not when it comes to cutesy semi-crude phrases like *sucks donkey balls*. No, then English is your whore. When Hamilton wants Anita to date *worm food*, watch the *idiot box*, and eat *shit on a shingle*, she's got it made. But sex? Then English isn't so helpful.

Onward, *chers lecteurs*. . . .

The most famous vampire of all, Bram Stoker's Count Dracula, followed in Lord Ruthven's tracks. He was a blue blood. He was cultured, had good manners, and conducted the proper sorts of gentlemanly business, like purchasing parcels of land that used to belong to the Church. He, too, was handsome and fascinating (although with "massive eyebrows") and traveled in high society. However, society—and language—had moved on a bit. Well, a *tiny* bit.

Though residing still in the land of skirted tables and chicken bearing "dark" and "white" meat instead of "legs" and "breasts," Dracula and his pursuers had at least moved up the symbolism scale from just teeth to other things, like needles. *Tres kinky!* No longer were characters penetrating the flesh of women with mere teeth! Science, in the person of Abraham Van Helsing, allowed them to do so with hollow metal tubes. And even though Stoker wrote his work in a pre-Freudian age, the symbolism is all too clear. Not even the thesaurus I consulted on the topic was fooled, as, in place of *needle*, it offered up *prick*. No subtlety there.

As Mina finds Lucy Westenra in a strange sleeping stupor in a cemetery, she reports that Lucy breathes in "long, heavy gasps" and she shudders and moans. Although a modern reader used to plain speaking might pass over this, no Victorian reader would be fooled. Dracula has, ah, *gone like a rat up a drainpipe*, as it were.

But Lucy is a she-devil who finds Victorian prudery and marriage laws so constricting that she complains that having one husband is not enough ("Why can't they let a girl marry three men, or as many as want her . . ."). And she will, by the time her head is chopped off, have been married by blood to no fewer than *five* husbands. Well, not legal husbands, but you understand what *symbolism* is, *mon cher*.

Van Helsing certainly understands symbolism, even if the rest of Stoker's putative heroes do not. He warns Seward, the second blood donor, "Mind, nothing must be said of this. If our young lover should turn up unexpected . . . It would at once frighten him and enjealous him." Sharing one woman among several men just ain't the Victorian idea of a proper relationship, but the idea sure made *Dracula's* original readers a bit breathless. Anita wouldn't know anything about that, of course (oh, wait . . .).

We must find a soft spot for poor Quincey Morris who, while symbolically wedded by a needle to the woman he loves, not only dies for her, but comes fifth out of five—after not only Lucy's fiancé, but a vampire, a madhouse doctor, and a seventy-year-old married Dutchman whose wife is a bit of a Bertha Rochester. Well, one can't have everything in love. That's something Anita grapples with continually in the series. And so does Nathaniel. And Richard. Just to name a few.

But forget just your ordinary, everyday lusts, needles substituting for penises, and crazy Dutchmen. Stoker even titillated his Victorian readers with hints of homoeroticism. When Jonathan Harker is attacked by three vampire women (Harker, ever conscious of class, notes clearly that they appear to be "ladies"), Dracula rescues Harker in a fury. Upon being charged by the women that he does not love, Dracula does something very curious: "Then the Count turned, after looking at my face attentively, and said in a soft whisper—'Yes, I too can love.'"

Mon dieu! It would appear that Dracula is perfectly willing to swing both ways, to fly the rainbow flag, to be a friend of Dorothy, at least with Harker. Now *that's* something Jean-Claude knows a thing or two about. In *Danse Macabre*, Asher tells Anita that, although he and Jean-Claude have been lovers and, indeed, look forward to being lovers again, "Jean-Claude would never be content *with just men in his bed*. He is a lover of women above all else."[1]

But he's a lover of men, too. Where Stoker only hinted around the subject with eyes averted, Hamilton screams it out loud, with eyes open and lights on. And while Anita is carnally entwined with Auggie and Jean-Claude in *Danse Macabre*, in full view of every preternatural creature in St. Louis. But when one decides to *go there*, one really needs to start assessing how much help and/or hindrance English is going to be.

As was explained to me by another writer long ago, "Think about it—is there really an uglier-sounding word in English than *vagina*?" Hmm, well, maybe *debacle*. Or *pustule*. Maybe.

The situation with *vagina* is bad enough that Eve Ensler felt compelled to write *The Vagina Monologues*, an entire play about women getting all sappy about their own anatomy. Though to be fair, they're celebrating the organ, not the word itself.

Still, the point is made: English lacks sexy words for sexy things. One can certainly engage in *bed boogie*, but honestly, would one really want to?

---

[1] Emphasis added.

Let's start with sex itself. One can *have sex* or *make love* and be talking about something relatively ordinary in a relatively polite way. Otherwise, you're going to have to go with something more clinical (*intercourse, penetration*), euphemistic (*sleep with, do*) or rude (*screw, fuck*). Not a whole lot of choice when you're going for erotic rather than clinical, boring, or rude. This paucity of words to describe the act, well, sucks. Hell, you want to set a *mood* for the readers, right? The sex shouldn't just be sex, it should lead to character development and plot development and be erotic at the same time. And if that isn't bad enough, it's got to be well-written.

Who'd set themselves up for that on purpose? Yeah, writers. Many of us aren't terribly bright sometimes.

Ah, *c'est la vie* . . . or *l'amour* . . . or *volupté*. And describing the act doesn't even begin to address the problem of what to do with the body parts. Well, not what to *do* with them, exactly, but what to call them.

If *vagina* just doesn't sound right, would *cunt* suit any better? Eh, too rude. How about *passage*? That one gets a lot of use, though not by Hamilton, and is accurate enough that it isn't even quite a euphemism. And let's not forget *glory hole*. Wait—on second thought, maybe we should. I'll forget it in favor of *snatch*, but, ah, well, that does reek of castration anxiety. How about scrapping all of those for *cooter*, even though that's a kind of turtle. Agreed?

Describing the rest of the lower female anatomy can either be scientific (*vulva, labia*) or downright puerile (*pink taco, hamster*). And then there's *beaver*, which, like *hamster*, begs the question of where all this castration anxiety comes from. I mean, equating a woman's genitals with something that bites? Calling Dr. Freud—stat!

Now when it comes to breasts, what can you say but *hooters, rack, girls, bazooms, tits, boobs, peaks, honeydews,* and *kalamazoos*? Actually, I sincerely hope the good folk of Kalamazoo don't realize the name of their town has been swiped and turned into such unrefined language. Or perhaps I should hope that they already knew that, so I am not the one responsible for popping their cherry.

At least when it comes to that phrase, *popping the cherry*, Hamilton is in the clear. She's already informed her readers that Anita had sex in college. When *Guilty Pleasures* opens, our heroine's no slut, but she's no virgin, either. Hamilton conveniently got herself out of any need to worry about *maidenheads*, *cherries*, or *removing the training wheels from the bicycle.*

Whew!

But truly, the main problem is what to call a penis, right? I mean, Anita's not worried about her own anatomy, and she's not gay or bi, so it's the male equipment that's going to be licked, sucked, stroked, and inserted. Tab A into Slot B, *n'est-ce pas?*

One of the more interesting things I've discovered lately is that you can't get a list of synonyms for *penis* from the online thesaurus. The same site that offered up *prick* for *needle* wants to know, rather primly, when quizzed about *penis*, "Did you mean *pen?*"

Ah, no, though seeing as how pens are long, straight, and hard, and can be held erect, I suppose that would work. Thanks, online thesaurus!

Pens aside, one of the perennial favorite alternate terms for penis is *phallus*, which has the bonus of sounding antique, and therefore it seems to work in historical fiction very well. But it's still kind of a silly word, not one I think Anita would have much patience with.

If the spam in my inbox is any indication, the words one should be using are *schlong, wang, fuckstick,* and/or *rod.* But those aren't really appealing. At least not to me, and I'll assume not so much to Hamilton (or Anita) either.

There's always the fallbacks of *johnson, dragon, snake, fireman,* or *johnny.* Hmm. Maybe not. And definitely not *cucumber of love, one-eyed trouser mouse,* or *purple-headed custard chucker,* all of which are completely absurd, and none of which I made up. Promise. Cross my heart, even.

Honestly, though, one of the best strategies for writing sex scenes is *not writing them.* Authors like Polidori and Stoker didn't get to show sex on stage, but perhaps their works were all the more erotic for that. Much as horror movies avoid showing the monster in the first reel, sexy tales that jump straight into bed have a tendency to just lie there like a, well, two-dollar whore. Part of the secret of erotic literature is to make the character, and the readers, wait.

Unfortunately, English isn't much help there, either. Terms like *foreplay* and *mutual sexual stimulation* are not only dull, but sound as if they belong in health class, not adult fiction. But there are other ways English can be useful. Hamilton chose to concentrate on what characters were wearing and, especially, how a voice could feel like velvet sliding up your spine. Hamilton's readers were introduced to Jean-Claude thusly:

> Softly curling hair tangled with the high white lace of an antique shirt. Lace spilled over pale, long-fingered hands. The shirt hung open, giving a glimpse of lean bare chest framed by more frothy lace. Most men couldn't have worn a shirt like that. The vampire made it seem utterly masculine. (*Guilty Pleasures*)

Now *that* is much more the thing, right? No dead gray eyes or leaden gazes or wan skin that refuses to warm to a blush, like Lord Ruthven. Or even, God forbid, overly bushy eyebrows, like Dracula. Nope, what we got right there in *Guilty Pleasures* was guys who could wear lace and make it masculine. Men who could whisper your name and make you shiver in a way you liked. Men who weren't going to need any penis substitutes like needles.

Men who had a way with words, and who weren't afraid to use them, despite their love interest's disinterest in being called *ma petite*.

Anita is taken enough with the vision of Jean-Claude in his lace shirt that she even finds herself wondering if the lace is as soft as it looks. Fortunately, she comes back from the brink—what kind of girl gives it up only three chapters into the first book in a series? English definitely has words for *that* sort.

The delicate tango between Anita and Jean-Claude does not culminate in sex for books upon books. Even two hundred pages into *The Killing Dance*, Anita is rejecting Jean-Claude's advances. He tells her, "your resistance to temptation grows thin," but even if that's true,

Anita still hasn't given up the fight. "No is one of my favorite words, Jean-Claude. You should know that by now."

Indeed, *no* remains in Anita's vocabulary for several more chapters, even though Jean-Claude "had the cutest butt I'd ever seen on a dead man."

The heart has reasons that reason cannot know, and all that. We knew Anita loved Jean-Claude. She also loved Richard. Heck, she was pretty good at being in love with lots of different men in different ways. Enough so that, eventually, there was going to be sex on stage. Even though The Rule said clearly, *No Sex On Stage*.

As Anita herself would say, dammit. Or perhaps she wouldn't. She's a very practical girl, and if you can stake someone on stage, why not do them on stage? Sounds fair.

Indeed, it was time, *cher lecteurs*. Foreplay can only go on for so long, and finally Anita came around to Jean-Claude's point of view. It was time to *give a dog a bone* or, perhaps, to *grease the wheel*.

Anita was ready. Jean-Claude was ready. The readers were ready. And even the English language was up to the task. Because when Anita falls into the bathtub with Jean-Claude in *The Killing Dance*, we are clear on what happens, but not treated to a litany of ridiculous words for anatomical parts.

> He was like carved alabaster, every muscle, every curve of his body pale and perfect. Telling him he was beautiful was redundant. Saying golly gee whiz seemed too uncool . . . I did what I wanted to do since I first saw him. I wrapped my fingers around him, squeezing gently . . . He pulled me against him suddenly, pressing our naked bodies together. The feel of him hard and firm against my stomach was almost overwhelming.

Now *that's* erotic and sexy. No Victorian sensibilities pandered to, no clichés utilized, no pet names or stilted description stumbled over. Language problems conquered, not just avoided. Readers are given an erotic sex scene that breaks Hamilton's own rule and leaves them wanting Anita again and again. And fortunately for them, she keeps on (ahem) coming. I doubt there's any stopping her.

As she'd say herself, golly gee whiz.

◆　　◆　　◆

Marella Sands is a native St. Louisan and member of the writers group Alternate Historians (www.sff.net/people/marella/). She earned degrees in anthropology from the University of Tulsa and Kent State University and currently teaches a class at Webster University on J. R. R. Tolkien. She has published both fiction and nonfiction. The author's household includes the author, her husband, a multitude of pet rats, and four cats.

Tragedy is easy, comedy is hard. I don't remember who said that, but it's true. It's much easier to make someone cry than to make them laugh. When I was a young pup in drama and doing work on stage I wanted to make people cry, or gasp. But the older I get the more I value laughter. I actually count how many laughs I get at question-and-answer sessions with the fans, and if I can make the audience both gasp in shock and then laugh, well, that's gold.

Cathy Clamp says that the Anita Blake books are funny and she's right. I'm not a humor writer by any means, I can't imagine trying to be funny for every page of an entire book, but there's always been humor in among the violence and sex in the Anita books. I learned a long time ago as a writer that if you hit someone with humor and then follow immediately with something horrible it doubles the impact. If you can make a reader laugh, then scream with terror, and then laugh again, you have nailed it. If you can do the scream, then the laugh, and then the scream, that is equally effective, because there is just something about breaking up the tension with humor and then raising the stakes that helps raise those stakes even higher. Sometimes the humor in my books is because I can't resist, and sometimes you laugh because it hurts too much to cry. The humor in Anita's world is a combination of outright funny, brave laughter in the face of sorrow, and that nervous laugh you do in the dark when you hear that noise behind you. That noise that you know shouldn't be there, and is probably nothing anyway, but you always have to turn, always have to look.

It is at these moments in the Anita books that I can never decide what kind of monster it should be: sexy, terrifying, or funny. Like real life sometimes you don't know whether to laugh, to cry, or to cure it all with a good roll in the hay. Or maybe that's just how I solve my problems?

—Laurell

Mom! There's Something Dead Sucking on My Neck!

CATHY CLAMP

> "Your breath smells like blood." [Nikolaos] jerked back, a hand going to her lips. It was such a human gesture that I laughed. . . . One small, slippered foot kicked me in the chest. The force tumbled me backwards, sharp pain, no air."
>
> —*Guilty Pleasures*

Laugh, scream, or sometimes both: that's our Anita Blake.

Like few authors before, Laurell K. Hamilton turned the burning light of reality on vampires and other denizens of the deepest recesses of our nightmares and showed us that even though they're born of darkness, powerful and vicious creatures could retain the humanity life gives: love, angst, sorrow, and even laughter. They aren't just terrifying; they can also be *funny*.

Much of the humor in the Anita Blake books comes from Anita's observations. She makes us think about the logic of vampires, and werewolves, and vampire executioners like nobody before. Why? Because as Anita so blithely tells us, "I could not stare down at the remains and not make jokes. I couldn't. I'd go crazy. Cops have the weirdest sense of humor because they have to" (*Laughing Corpse*). But while she uses her wry wit and sarcastic view of the world to cope, she does something for us, too—something more than just make us laugh. To accuse a centuries-old vampire of bad breath and have that vampire *react* to the insult brings Anita's alternate reality closer to our own. It makes her world seem more real.

So let's take a closer look at the humor in Anita's world. There's no lack of ammo to choose from whenever Anita needs a good barb to keep her enemies off-balance . . . but we'll offer a few more, and in the meantime, get a little deeper into her world.

Let's start with bad breath. You have to admit, a vampire's life must have quite literally *sucked* before toothpaste and breath mints. Shortly after Anita encounters Jean-Claude for the first time in *Guilty Pleasures*, he whispers a question to the audience at the club. He asks whether we've ever wished to feel his breath upon our skin. Skin, yes. But *nose*? Even Jean-Claude's looks could only get him so far in today's hyper-hygienic world.

Thank goodness for the ability to bespell your victims. Do you suppose new vampires have to practice bespelling? Willie McCoy tries and fails to bespell Anita in *Guilty Pleasures*: "You're the new dead, Willie. Vampire or not, you've got a lot to learn." I'd imagine learning to bespell would be like practicing an important speech. But who would volunteer to be the "audience" while you practiced? *You desire me. I'm beautiful. Your greatest wish is to have me bite you.* No, wait. She flinched. Maybe not *bite*. Hmm . . . how about *kiss*? Yeah, that sounds better. Aw, man! She's shivering when I touch her. That's not my fault. That stupid coffin was freezing! *Oh, and forget how cold and clammy my hands are.* No, that sounds lame. *You're warm . . . so hot, burning up. You want my hands to cool you off. You need it . . . need me. So desperate for cold.* Good. Totally Dracula-like. She's smiling again and I'm close enough to smell the blood under her skin. Open mouth, bare fangs. Geez, now she's wrinkling her nose and pulling away! I knew I should have stolen the Certs out of that last guy's pocket. *Ignore your nose. It's just the scent of your own desire.*

Humans are so picky today it's amazing we ever managed to procreate before bathing and dental hygiene became common. And it's not just vampires who likely have the problem. There are other creatures in Anita's world that subsist on blood and meat: werewolves and wererats, plus lions, tigers, and bears—oh my! It can't be any easier for them to keep kissable-fresh. Protein has an annoying habit of breaking down, whether or not it's located in an enzyme-producing mouth. Those of you who own outdoor cats will especially understand. When you spot a scattering of feather fluff on the ground, or the unrecognizable remains of what used to be something small and furry on the porch, kitty should not be encouraged to breathe near your face for a few days. Death leaves a certain lingering . . . *fragrance* that doesn't invite close contact.

Speaking of hunting for food, I have to admit to a certain level of sympathy for vampires. Imagine waking for the evening with all the speed and grace of a turtle on tranquilizers. I fully understand why Jean-Claude made Jason his *pomme de sang*. Jason's casual comment, "Sometimes he likes a snack when he first wakes up," in *Bloody Bones* belies a hard truth of being undead; the living can outrun you before you warm up. I'd imagine the waking ritual is somewhat different for a vampire who's not master of a city and doesn't have a handy werewolf to snack on. When the sun dips below the horizon and the sky turns a rich indigo, the Regular-Joe vampire wakes. He's hungry and cranky and wants nothing more than to warm his flesh . . . presently the same temperature as his quiet, secure, *unheated* underground crypt. Oh, sure—he probably took off the bloodstained shirt before bed, flossed the stubborn stains from between his fangs, and snuck in a shower before he died at dawn, so at least he was clean when he woke up. But unless he's as fortunate as Jean-Claude and has a willing snack coffin-side, he's got to go hunting. Personally, making coffee before I've *had* my coffee is hard enough, without having to go chase down the machine in the front yard and wrestle it to the ground.

I mean, c'mon . . . that's just *cruel*!

It's difficult to even conceive how it might have been to be a vampire before the landmark decision of *Addison v. Clark* in Anita's reality that "gave us a revised version of what life was, and what death wasn't" (*Guilty Pleasures*). Moving like a lizard in December, dragging my bloodless body out into the darkness to wait for someone to show up or going into public to bespell someone would make me want to go back to my coffin and hit the snooze alarm. I wouldn't be a very good vampire.

I'd do better as a shapeshifter. They can just order a hamburger at a fast food joint, or a rare sirloin at a steakhouse . . . all without raising suspicion. Even a shifter the size of a pony could get away with murder and explain it away easily to nosy neighbors—no telltale weapons to hide: "Raina sliced through the bloody apron. Two quick, hard slices. The clothes underneath were untouched" (*The Lunatic Café*). As a bonus, you can use your pets as scapegoats. Dig up your own back yard to bury your kill? Bad Fido! Track blood across the carpeting? Oh, that cat's always dragging something inside. Then it's just a quick trip to the all-night grocery across town for a rental steam cleaner. No fuss, no muss. There are no coffins to hide, you can mow at midday like the rest of the block, and you don't have to avoid wooden furnishings that could become stake-fodder. It's a snap to convince your friends that stainless steel is trendy—a less toxic substitute for silver tableware at Christmas.

Even small private dinners tend to put odd behavior in the spotlight, but I think public gatherings would be the hardest part. For a vampire, being squarely under the suspicious gaze of the common citizen would be frustrating. People stare at pale people—either you're a computer geek who has spent way too much time in front of a monitor, or you're a vampire. Both are high on the avoidance list for the nightclub crowd . . . which is where I'd imagine most victims come from, judging by the scene in Jean-Claude's place, described in *Guilty Pleasures*: "The room was full of liquor and laughter, and a few faked screams as the vampire waiters moved around the tables. There was an undercurrent of fear. That peculiar terror that you get on roller coasters and at horror movies. Safe terror." Beer-goggles could easily take the place of bespelling before that crucial first meal, and drunk people aren't terribly careful about who they leave bars with. Even when their partners for the night are oddly pale people with a tendency toward lace.

Let's talk about clothes for a minute. Lace seems to be a mainstay for Jean-Claude, and you have to wonder why. I have a lovely lace tablecloth, hand-crafted a hundred years ago. It takes constant maintenance to keep it nice. It yellows even in a darkened drawer and can gather stains from food eaten in a different zip code. As clothing, lace scratches and gets caught on nearly everything. But at least with white lace, skin pallor isn't so noticeable, so that's something. Either vampires are the ultimate clotheshorses with a *lot* of money to update their wardrobes, or they use a lot of vampire illusion magic to keep people from noticing the untidy dark dots that stubbornly remain after washing.

Of course, in the early days, before *Addison v. Clark*, I'm sure vampires simply took what they needed or wanted to make life comfortable. But after legality, life must have become more difficult. I found it interesting, as an admittedly amateur student of economics, how many of the undead in Anita's world are employed, and what that might mean for the economy in that alternate reality. Jean-Claude owns a string of businesses. He even has a corporate jet. But I suppose if undead isn't really *dead* in the eyes of the law, lots of things vampires thought they'd escaped probably came back to haunt them. The owner of the abandoned house at the edge of town where you'd hidden your coffin is not only no longer afraid, he's now charging *rent*. Even the grave can't get you away from that blasted alimony ruling, and no doubt the credit card companies had a field day in court!

Anita herself fights for the rights of zombies, to keep them from being abused by unscrupulous business owners looking to save a buck on payroll. But surely zombies in the kitchen and vampires working the night shift must have lowered the employment possibilities for new graduates. And are people who die at age fifty-nine and come back as vampires exempt from mandatory retirement? Does the

Americans with Disabilities Act apply? Are the *living* the new disabled in Anita's world? Is showing up for a job interview with a rosy complexion now a detriment? Stock up on that pale make-up, kids! You'll need it to get any use out of that diploma.

In Anita's world, make-up to look like a vampire is probably more easily found through L'Oreal or M.A.C. than the local Halloween provider, thanks to Belle Morte's line of vampires and how they turned the whole concept of what vampires were supposed to look like on its ear. The vampires in Anita's life, at least, have had "drop-dead gorgeous" applied at a new level.

Vampires were really the world's first plastic surgeons. Want to keep your youthful good looks? We have the answer! All nip, no tuck. Never mind the small side effects: the pale, pasty skin, the glowing eyes, the teeth that ruin the thousands spent on braces. You can still show off those perfect abs and chiseled jaw to the girls . . . and the beaches aren't as crowded at night.

Not *all* vampires are pretty, of course. In Anita's world, even the average Regular-Joe human can get bumped up to vamp by getting bumped off. Take Willie McCoy, for example. He's no prize in the looks department. He's also not tough, nor particularly bright.

That's another thing. While getting turned into a vampire by one of Belle Morte's line can do wonders for you in the looks department, there's no help for being dumb. Despite their many years on earth as the undead, vampires are surprisingly dim. Maybe it's the simultaneous death of all those brain cells when they're turned. Because if a smart vampire bared his teeth at a woman and she continued to walk toward him, looking confident, he *should* be pulling the ranged arsenal out from under his cloak before she gets one step closer. Anita would have been dead a dozen times over if the vamps she faced had just been smart enough to carry a gun. The world has changed from a thousand, or even a hundred, years ago. It's perfectly okay for a male vampire, or a shapeshifter, to shoot at the woman intent on ending his existence. A stun grenade will take the starch out of a species-discriminating killer's smile, and let's see a lowly human, no matter how well-armed, drive a stake through a vampire's heart after a clip from an UZI takes off that arm below the elbow. I'm always surprised there aren't more fanged Edwards in Anita's world.

If I were a vampire in Anita's world, I'd buy a few Kevlar vests with ceramic breastplates. It wouldn't stop a determined vampire killer forever, but the longer they have to fumble around getting it off, the better the chance the sun will set before they do. I'd also order a special coffin, lined with asbestos shingles—no lungs (well, no *working* lungs), no lung cancer. Heck, while we're at it, the lid should be made of solid lead. Vampires are strong, but it would be too heavy for one mere human to lift, and even if that human brought friends, a lead lid might crush their little skulls before they could get their implements of destruction prepared. Kevlar is a good idea for the shifters out there, too—they've already proven their effectiveness on police dogs. Buy a Christmas gift from the heart this year: a silver-deflecting vest for the werewolf in your life will guarantee he or she will be around to slaver affection on you next full moon.

Those microchip implants probably wouldn't be a bad idea either. Instead of the owner's name, they could list the shifters' daytime identity and address. And as a bonus, it'd make it a lot easier to keep track of the less than law-abiding. The chicken ranch owner who wakes up to a pile of feathers could use high-tech readers attached to their security systems to identify the werewolf who jumped the fence. Then it's a simple matter of sending a bill. Maybe a similar system would work for vampires. Bespelling a woman into opening her window so you can suck her dry would lead the police straight to your crypt the next morning. If only humans smartened up!

Then again, if the vamps and werewolves and humans got smarter, what would we need Anita for? And not having Anita around anymore would be a shame. Looking at Hamilton's alternate St. Louis through Anita's eyes uncovers a thousand brilliant bits of comedy gold, from the occasional absurdities of the *ardeur* to imagining the great and terrible Jean-Claude rolling on the floor savoring the flavor of blackberries through Anita's tongue. I look forward to a hundred more stories from Ms. Hamilton about Anita's world—all colored by that special brand of sarcasm that's made Anita as infamous in her world as she is in our own.

◆   ◆   ◆

Cathy Clamp is the *USA Today* bestselling author of the Sazi shapeshifter series and Thrall Vampire series for Tor Books, along with co-author C. T. Adams. They have also begun to write urban fantasy novels as Cat Adams for Tor with a new vampire/siren series called the Blood Singer debuting in June 2010. She is an avid fan of the Anita Blake reality, as well as pretty much every other urban fantasy series out there. When she's not writing (or reading), she's up to her ears in projects with her husband on their small goat farm in the beautiful Texas Hill Country. She can be visited online at http://catadams.net, is happy to visit with fans and friends on Twitter and Myspace as cathyclamp, or is musing at her and C. T.'s joint blog http://catadamsauthor.blogspot.com.

Battle not with monsters, lest ye become a monster,
and if you gaze into the abyss, the abyss gazes also into you.
—Friedrich Nietzsche

That quote is at the heart of the Anita Blake series for me now, but why that quote began to mean so much to me was because I researched the real world for the books. I talked to police, ex-military, and finally researched serial killers. (The police and the military men and women who were so generous with their time and knowledge, I thank you all. The books would not be what they are without you.)

I have a close friend whom I met when he was a rookie. He believed he would save the world. He was so bright and shiny and eager. Ten years later I've watched the brightness dim and the shiny wear away. I learned through him that you can't catch all the bad guys, there are too many of them. I learned that after a decade you begin to value going home alive to your family more than any arrest you will make. That saving a life means more than putting a bad guy away, even though you understand that having the bad guy behind bars means he won't be hunting any more victims.

Cynical doesn't begin to cover what he and I have become over the last ten years of friendship. I have been the person he could tell anything to over the years. He was the one who taught me that the greatest gift you can give to the men and women in uniform is to listen. To simply listen, and not show shock, or fear, or God forbid repulsion. To let them know that you are their quiet pool that they can drop their horror into and know that it won't come back and bite them, that they can tell you anything and it's okay. (It helps that I seem to share a cop sense of humor. Dark humor: no one does it better than the police, unless it's emergency room personnel. But my money is on the cops.) I have had ex-military and police tell me what it feels like to take a human life in the line of duty. Their honesty over the years shaped Anita Blake, shaped my writing, and in the end it shaped me.

But the research that took the most of whatever innocence I had still lingering was the serial killer research. Knowing that one human being can do that to another forever changed how I look at people. I have learned things I did not want to know. I know now that no matter how horrible my idea is for fiction that real people have already done far worse. That is simple truth. In fact, I have a rule that I never do any violence in my books that can be done without my world's "magic system," unless it's something that is based on a real crime. If some killer has already done it then I can put it in my books, but if it's something I've never heard anyone else really do, I won't write about it. I won't feed the real monsters because they don't need my help. They are creative on their own.

Think about what I said just now. Anything that's ever happened in my books that can be done without my preternatural stuff is based on real crime, real things that real people did to other real, live people. That should scare you more than any fiction I will ever write.

◆

◆

◆

—Laurell

The Other Side of the Street

Anita Blake and the Horror Renaissance

ALASDAIR STUART

There's an image that always springs to mind when someone mentions horror to me. It's the traditional mob of angry villagers making their way up the hill toward Castle McGuffin where the Thing That Should Not Be lives. Sometimes it's a vampire, sometimes it's Frankenstein's Monster, but the mob remain the same. They're all carrying pitchforks and burning torches, they're all peasants, they're all angry, they're all frightened, and they're all men.

From the story of Mary Shelley's doomed monster down to Doctor Loomis in the Halloween series, it has fallen, time and again, to the male characters to root out evil and horror, to drag it shrieking into the light and, frequently, away from the helpless females it's been trying to eat, marry, or occasionally both. Horror isn't just about watching something approach, as William Friedkin, director of *The Exorcist*, famously said; it's frequently about watching a man set fire to it or shove a stake through its heart.

But just as male characters have traditionally hogged the limelight while simultaneously soaking it in blood, female characters have gradually evolved from victims to something much more interesting. It's a process that began in *Dracula*, where both Lucy and Mina are extremely cognizant that something is being done to them but lack the knowledge to understand it and, by extension, defend themselves against it. Later on, characters like Laurie Strode and Sydney Prescott, the endlessly troubled heroines of the Halloween and Scream franchises, are gifted with that knowledge, and in Sydney's case manage to recognize not only their situation but how to manipulate it to their own ends. Over time, it's become clear that the female characters' perspective is much more interesting than their male counterparts'; the men see something unspeakable from a distance, but the women see it up close, and in doing so, inevitably, gain a better understanding of it. It's this understanding that lies at the heart not only of Anita Blake, but of the impact she's had on the horror genre as a whole.

Anita is a new kind of heroine. She has the intellectual and emotional investment of Mina Harker as well as the physical prowess of Buffy Summers, but for the first time she combines them, uses them as tools to understand the world she lives in instead of simply destroying it. In short, while Anita is fully capable of killing monsters, she finds it almost impossible not to understand them. She's both a monster hunter and a monster, a woman not just working in, but changing, a man's world. She's something new and, crucially, something indicative of a major shift in horror as a genre. Up is down, black is white, and the lynch mob may well be monsters themselves.

Compare Anita to a character like Dolph Storr, the head of the RPIT Unit Anita consults for in the early novels. Dolph is a fascinating character in himself and one who, in a kinder world, would be the hero of his own story. He is a relentlessly effective police officer, a good boss, a husband and father, and as a result is every inch the traditional male hero. He's a good man in a world that as far as he's concerned is going to hell, and that only makes him cling to his goodness, to define himself by it even more. He should be, when viewed in these terms, Anita's rock, her moral compass. Instead, as the novels continue he is pushed further and further to the outskirts of the series, as he finds it more and more difficult to accept the gradual intermingling of the various species—especially when it's revealed his son Darrin has married a vampire. Anita, in contrast, embraces it. The direct, brash re-animator of *Guilty Pleasures* is a very different person than the fiercely capable, ruthless necromancer of the later books. As events pull her more and more into contact with the monsters she started off the series investigating, Anita embraces the possibilities for change and growth it offers her.

Anita is able to do so as effectively as she does for a reason. Her abilities first manifest during her adolescence, the time of life most closely associated with emotional and physical change, and this provides her with the first step toward her adult view of the preternatural, as something which is as commonplace, as familiar as everything else in her life. This subversion of the mundane and use of the normal as a carrier for the supernatural is a recurrent theme throughout Anita's life and one Hamilton explores with tremendous gusto. Time and again, every element of Anita's life that could be considered normal—such as a job, friends, and relationships—is driven back to the preternatural, the other, the alien.

Anita lives in a world where the monster isn't just under the bed, there's a good chance he delivered it. This is where the feminine perspective really comes into its own as we suddenly find ourselves looking at the world not through the lens of physical superiority that the male subconscious is equipped with, but with the constant, rolling threat-assessment of the female subconscious. For the horror heroine, potential danger is everywhere, and for all her abilities, all her politicking, all her partners, it's all Anita can do to keep one step ahead of the countless dangers she's surrounded by. While Anita eventually comes to accept her distance from humanity, she still keeps one eye on the people she chooses to spend her life with.

Anita not only recognizes her differences, she relishes them, turns them inward and uses them as tools and weapons instead of burdens to bear. She's aware that she's different, aware that she's not quite different enough, and crucially, aware of how useful that last realization can be.

A lesser character would simply visit this metaphorical dark side of the street, this place where morality is negotiable and alliances are as important as friendships. This is the place inhabited by the werewolves and vampires of supernatural fiction and the desperate, lonely criminals and police officers of crime fiction. It's also the place Raymond Chandler talks about in his iconic quote:

> Down these mean streets a man must go who is not him-
> self mean, who is neither tarnished nor afraid. The detec-
> tive must be a complete man and a common man and yet
> an unusual man. He must be, to use a rather weathered
> phrase, a man of honor. He talks as the man of his age
> talks, that is, with rude wit, a lively sense of the grotesque,
> a disgust for sham, and a contempt for pettiness.

Anita doesn't just walk down Chandler's mean streets, she lives on them, shops on them, and dates on them as well. This is a woman who lives in two pairs of worlds: the normal and the preternatural, horror and crime. In many ways she's a PI in the wrong genre, a woman who balances compassion and intellect with physicality in a very similar way to Val McDermid's Kate Brannigan or Liza Cody's Eva Wylie. Anita, while steeped in the preternatural world, is able to see through and past it to deal with people as individuals, and do so with "rude wit" and an extremely "lively sense of the grotesque." Where Dolph sees something to be feared and destroyed, sees the blank white face of Lon Chaney or Peter Lorre dancing just beyond the torchlight, Anita sees the fear in their eyes, the desperation in their actions. She's compassionate and open and drawn to them as her people, even as she's checking exits and making sure she knows where her weapons are. But as Anita becomes more and more caught up in the world outside the light, she begins to wonder which side of the street she really belongs on. And so she—both literally and met-aphorically—steps out into the darkness, faces the monster down, and does the one thing the mob can't or won't do: meets the monster on *its* terms. As a result, the very nature of horror, as presented in the books, changes. Horror has often been about absence, about see-ing something awful just beyond the light of the campfire. Shelley's monster, Lovecraft's deathless elder gods, Halloween's Michael My-ers, the Gentlemen of *Buffy's* "Hush," and the demons of *Supernatural* all operate within this principle, and are all denizens of the other side of the street, of the place most of us would prefer not to go and would rather not think about. Don't leave the campfire; don't go off somewhere to make out; never ever say you'll "be right back." These have been the touchstones of horror for so long that they've not only become an unofficial gospel but have directly led to the boom in self-referential horror in the nineties. The half-glimpsed form in the darkness became a merchandising leviathan, and as horror stepped out into the light it began to change on an almost primal level, beginning with the meta-textual, self-referential *Scream* series and moving through mainstream parodies to the bizarre, splintered set of sub-genres cinematic horror is today.

This is where Anita is an actively subversive figure, the first one through the door and out into a world that sits next to ours but doesn't play by the same rules. Her eventual willingness to embrace what lives in the shadows not only changes her but changes *it*, dragging it out into the light and giving the bogeyman edges, a face, a name, a personality. This willingness to stare darkness in the face and, if needed, buy it a drink has led to a sea change that has been felt through much of contemporary horror. After decades of the masculine viewpoint being dominant and the monster being something to be feared and destroyed, the feminine viewpoint has taken control, and now the monster is something to understand first and destroy, if necessary, second. At first glance, this newfound normalcy robs traditional monsters of much of their menace and, more importantly, their charm. But as the Anita Blake novels progress, the usual trappings of vampires and lycanthropes largely fall away, and they become something more than the stereotype, something more interesting than pantomime fangs and fake furry hands: people. Each of the supporting cast are revealed to have their own agendas, their own traumas, and their own perspectives on events in Anita's increasingly complicated life. The transformation of Jean-Claude is a particularly good example of this. Initially set up as an antagonist, he goes so far as using threats against the life of Richard Zeeman, Anita's first lycanthrope partner, to get her to date him in *The Lunatic Café*. He's a curious figure, one part Machiavellian politician and one part tragic antihero, and it's only as the novels go on that we begin to learn why he is the way he is. Jean-Claude feels tremendous affection for his friends but is all too aware of the appalling danger that places them in. As a result, he walls himself off from everyone but those closest to him in order to protect them. His attraction to Anita flies in the face of this practice, and trying to figure out whether that attraction is born from his recognition of her power or genuine love makes for fascinating reading. Superficially, Jean-Claude is a monster, but as the series goes on we discover his motivations, which makes him become one of the series' most sympathetic characters. He's still a monster but, as Anita and the reader learn together, monsters can be just as complicated as people.

It's this newfound depth that not only replaces the traditional bogeyman approach but also, almost overnight, completely changes the landscape of horror fiction. The idea that the monsters are as complicated and interesting as we are isn't a new one, but embracing it to this degree certainly is, and it leads to some fascinating, challenging stories both within the series and beyond it. The monster becomes someone you pass on the street, and that acceptance replaces uncertainty as the basis of fear. Ivy, in Kim Harrison's Rachel Morgan series, is both a fascinating, beautiful woman and something so unutterably alien that Rachel has trouble being in the same room with her for much of the first book. Likewise, in the Sookie Stackhouse novels by Charlaine Harris, and especially in the TV adaptation *True Blood*, what makes Bill the vampire genuinely terrifying isn't his undead status but the fact that he's a polite, charming Southern gentlemen. The monsters look like us, they talk like us, they have the same desires as us, but that familiarity is laced with something attractive, inhuman, and incredibly dangerous.

But for all that danger, all the monsters Anita walks with, works with, and sleeps with, one of the largest dangers she faces is a human she's forced to work with. Olaf, introduced in *Obsidian Butterfly*, is arguably the series' first truly monstrous protagonist. A former intelligence officer, Olaf is a serial murderer and rapist retained by the U.S. government on the condition that he keeps most of his sprees outside the country's borders. With his single-minded rage and need to commit violence, Olaf is at least as savage, if not more so, than the preternatural characters of the series, a hulking embodiment of death who becomes obsessed by hunting with—or simply hunting—Anita. He's the embodiment of physical danger, a permanently cocked trigger with no regard for human life, and Anita's reaction to him shows exactly how well developed her instincts have become: "A part of me screamed, kill him now. the rest of me really didn't disagree with that little voice" (*The Harlequin*). If any character would be fodder for the traditional horror lynch mob, it's Olaf. But even here, Hamilton refuses to let her characters off easily. Olaf has just enough education to perform, just enough awareness to realize what he is and that, on some level, Anita represents an opportunity for him to change. Olaf is a monster, that's a given; but he's a monster who sees himself differently through Anita, and in doing so, he has the potential to change for the better. Whether that's possible or even acceptable is unclear, but what isn't is Anita's stoic, grounded refusal to take the easy way out and hate Olaf unconditionally. She's been on the dark side of the street for too long and can see far too well to allow herself that luxury.

There is, of course, a second possibility: that Olaf is drawn to Anita the same way she was drawn to Jean-Claude, as a predator recognizing its place in the food chain and and feeling both a fear of and attraction to the more powerful creatures above it. Viewed this way, it becomes clear that the changes Anita undergoes across the series aren't just in response to the threats she encounters but are threats in and of themselves. Anita may feel distanced from humanity, but she understands that distance and is aware of what it implies: that Dolph may be right, that she may be willingly surrendering her humanity to a world of monsters wearing beautiful masks. It's a complex, uneasy question that provides a backdrop of tension to the later books in particular and places the whole series in a very different and potentially very disturbing light. Because, in the end, for all her hard work and training, the biggest threat to Anita may be Anita herself.

In fact, looked at in further detail, there's some compelling circumstantial evidence for this. She buries herself in the preternatural, and the world she finds there (and one reading of the books) is that she does so to embrace the only part of the world that has ever truly embraced her. Another reading is that Anita surrounds herself with monsters not only because that's the only place she feels at home, but because she's afraid monsters are the only people that can stop her if she ever grows too powerful. The most compelling thought speaks to her pragmatic nature: that Anita wants to feel comfortable, to accept herself and be accepted. She walks in the dark because that's where the answers lie, and she makes the sacrifices she does with the understanding, and the hope, that she won't have to do so forever.

Regardless of her reasons, Anita Blake was one of the first characters to walk across the street, to not only understand the monsters but actively question them, connect with them, and, in doing so, understand them. She's a catalyst, a figure around whom immense narrative change has coalesced and led to some of the most interesting developments in modern horror, part of a new wave who have taken the genre largely for their own and changed it for the better. In doing so, Anita has faced down and killed the one monster that is truly unreasoning, unthinking, and savagely and randomly violent: Anita Blake has been instrumental in the death of the lynch mob, banishing them back to their village forever and letting the Things That Should Not Be out into the light. It may not be a safer world, but thanks to Anita and Laurell K. Hamilton, it's a far more interesting one.

◆   ◆   ◆

Alasdair Stuart is the host of Pseudopod (www.pseudopod.org), the winner of the 2009 Parsec Award for Best Speculative Fiction Magazine or Anthology Podcast. He edits Hub (www.hubfiction.com), a free weekly PDF genre fiction magazine, and his nonfiction has appeared in *The Guardian*, *Neo*, *Death Ray*, *Sci Fi Now*, and many more. He blogs for *SFX* (www.sfx.co.uk) and *Bleeding Cool* (www.bleedingcool.com) and is an active roleplaying game writer, currently hard at work on material for the official *Doctor Who* Roleplaying Game. He lives in the north of England with his wife and not quite enough models of the TARDIS.

This essay was full of surprises and insights for me as a writer. I had never realized how much Richard's squeamishness at being the best werewolf he can be pushes Anita time and again into being a better monster than he is to save him, save others, save herself. And protecting those weaker than you is my measure for worth; of course, my judgment of what constitutes weaker may not be everyone's.

As for Jean-Claude growing as a character from the beginning, I never thought I wrote vampire novels. I always wrote novels about people who happened to be vampires, or werewolves, or necromancers. I could never sit down and think, *I'll write a story about vampires*, without thinking what would it do to a person to be immortal, ageless, always beautiful, super strong, super fast, able to control the minds of other people, and needing to see other human beings as food. What would that do to you as a person? What would it do to you in a century? Two centuries? Longer? What would that do to your character? That was how I created Jean-Claude, and Asher, and all the other vampires in my world. First they must be people, and only second anything else.

The exceptions to that are, strangely, my human characters like Edward and Olaf. They were created to be perfect killers, and only slowly did they reveal more to me. Edward especially has surprised the hell out of me over the years. I didn't learn about the fiancée and the kids until about two sentences before Anita did in *Obsidian Butterfly*. You could have knocked me over with the proverbial feather. Olaf was supposed to be a serial killer and a true monster, but even he has surprised me. He's still one of the scariest characters I've ever created, but the fact that he has female fans that want him and Anita to become a couple creeps me more than my fictional killer. High eww factor.

Micah was originally supposed to be a villain and a huge betrayal for Anita, but from the moment he stepped on stage he refused to be a bad guy. From the first moment he saw Anita he saw in her safety and a home for him and his wereleopard pard, and he was willing to do anything, anything, to have that with her. Anita needed a helpmate, a true partner, and in Micah she found it.

But Natasha is right that it's been Nathaniel who has done more to domesticate Anita than any other man in her life. In fact Natasha made some points about the evolution of their relationship that I hadn't quite seen myself. The best nonfiction about your own work makes you rethink it, and go, oh, of course. It wasn't just Anita that didn't see how she felt about Nathaniel for books; I didn't see it either. I guess for a real-life parallel my husband, Jonathon, and I thought we were just friends long after all of our friends knew we were more. We argued for a long time that we were just friends. Anita and I argued for a long time that we didn't love Nathaniel, couldn't love him. Methinks the lady doth protest too much, and so does the author.

Most poignant for me was Natasha quoting the dialogue from *Incubus Dreams* where Anita is willing to sacrifice everyone but Nathaniel. I honestly didn't see that then, and so how could Anita have a clue, if I didn't? Sometimes your characters are more real than even you understand; they sort of sneak up on you, and take your hand and lead you to domestic bliss that you never planned for your main character, and make you wistful for a wife of your own. Jonathon and I both agree that having a third who is more domestically talented would be swell, it's just the emotional upkeep that makes Anita and me wonder at that whole extra person. In real life there are no rewrites tomorrow after the fight today.

—Laurell

The Domestication of a Vampire Executioner

NATASHA FONDREN

Anita Blake is a monster killer, a sometimes murderer, a once-in-awhile torturer. She's an executioner of vampires—the shortest executioner of vampires in the United States—but don't let that fool you: Anita Blake has the highest kill count of any vampire executioner in the nation, possibly the world. And that's just counting the *legal* kills.

She's not exactly someone you want to take home and introduce to your mother, someone you imagine making dinner, walking the dog, or dropping the kids off at soccer practice. She's been called a sociopath, a zombie queen, and coffin bait. She's a necromancer, a master vampire (somehow without really being a vampire), a succubus, and the human servant of the Master of the City.

She is not your girl next door.

And she doesn't want to be. She never has. At the beginning of the series, Anita prefers coming home to an empty apartment when she's done raising the dead for the night. It's quiet there: peaceful and private. She can wash off the goat's blood and the zombie goo with a hot shower, cuddle with her stuffed penguin, enjoy having a kitchen she doesn't cook in—a kitchen no one cooks in.

Her ideal pets? *Fish.* As she says: "You don't walk them, pick up after them, or have to housebreak them. Clean the tank occasionally, feed them, and they don't give a damn how many hours of overtime you work" (*The Laughing Corpse*).

No one knows what happens to the pet fish. They disappear in later books. They never die and then swim into her bed sheets, which is better luck than Anita's had with past pets, like the dead dog that crawled in her bed while she was sleeping. Or the road kill that her powers accidentally animated, and the dead-by-suicide professor who knocked on her dorm room door.

And she doesn't just raise the dead; she executes the undead.

Anita Blake believes it is her life's mission to save the world from the monsters: the werewolves and the vampires and the demons. She is anything but a candidate for domestication. Like the cats she carries in her bloodstream, she is wild, unable to be tied down or put behind a fence, white or otherwise.

And yet, as the series goes on, she *is* domesticated. As she starts protecting the monsters she once sought to destroy, as she starts loving the monsters she once thought had no emotions, she learns it is safe to soften around those you love.

In the end, it is the wild monsters who tame Anita, who show her how to love, and who give her the comfort of home and family and togetherness.

It Takes a Monster to Catch a Monster

> "I've become one of the monsters, and if it will save Richard's family, I am happy to be one."
>
> "Feel any better?" Jason said.
>
> "Yeah, I do. I'm a monster, but it's for a good cause."
>
> —*Blue Moon*

In the beginning, domestication is something Anita thinks she hopes for and aspires to. She longs for a normal life, for a safe life, for a life free of monsters and demons and all the things that go bump in the night. When Anita first meets Richard, she likes him because of his normalcy, because she believes he is not a monster. To Anita, Richard is the white-picket-fence dream, the man she turns to when she longs for a life free of killing and death and preternatural responsibilities. Ironically, in the end, it is Richard's desire to be free of the monster world that drives Anita further into it.

Very soon after their first date, Anita learns that Richard is a werewolf. She likes him for his humanity, but the fact that he's a monster freaks her out. Can she help it that, when they go to a restaurant, she wonders if he wants to eat the elderly couple at the next table? That she suspects him of eating Little Red Riding Hood? Sure, she reminds herself that lycanthropy is a disease, like AIDS. She reminds herself that it is not right to be prejudiced.

As she rationalizes, it's not because he's a monster that she doesn't want to have sex with Richard: it's because she does not engage in pre-marital sex. She was raised Catholic. So when he proposes, she accepts. It made sense, for a moment: she craves normal; she craves life; she even craves sex. Because he craves the same things, Richard represents domestication to Anita, in spite of the fact that he is a werewolf.

But Anita regrets the engagement instantly. At first, she wrestles with whether or not Richard is human. He is the closest she'll ever get to the two-car garage and the two-point-five kids, but still, she worries about the morality of marrying a monster. Even though he caught lycanthropy through a vaccine and no fault of his own, she blames his beast for her hesitation. If he were human, she thinks, maybe things would be different.

At this point in the series, though, Richard is solid white-picket-fence material. So where does Anita's fear of marriage come from? Why the resistance to domestication? It is, after all, what she thought she wanted.

Perhaps Anita's extreme reaction to him cooking in her kitchen is a clue. When she comes home to her apartment after a rough night, she's upset to find music playing: it's not quiet. He's left the door unlocked. He's in her kitchen. In an *apron*. She runs to her room to make sure there are no signs of an "invasion." The romantic dinner with candles upsets her so much that he clears the evidence away while she is in the shower. As she frets about the situation, she starts to wonder if her hesitations may be rooted in something other than his being a werewolf:

> Did Richard have this domestic vision of a little house, him in the kitchen, me working, and kids? Oh, damn, we were going to have to sit down and have a serious talk. If we did manage to get engaged like normal people, what did that mean? Did Richard want children? I certainly didn't. Where would we live? My apartment was too small. His house? I wasn't sure I liked that idea. It was his house. Shouldn't we have our house? Shit. Kids, me? Pregnant, me? Not in this lifetime. I thought furriness was our biggest problem. Maybe it wasn't. (*The Lunatic Café*)

When she's confronted with the normal life she thought she wanted, Anita instantly realizes that it is not for her. She believes the monsters live in a world too dangerous for normalcy: the work she does would put neighbors and human friends in harm's way. But her desire to protect humans from monsters is not her reason for giving up on a normal life; it's her excuse. The moment she realizes what normal would entail, the grass no longer becomes greener on the other side.

Abandoning a normal life, however, means she's left without a community. She can't live in the regular world, and up until *The Killing Dance*, her prejudice against the monsters keeps her from living fully in their world, too: she'll only kill in their world. As Richard bitterly points out, "You don't sleep with me, either, because I'm a monster, too. But you can kill us, can't you, Anita? You just can't fuck us" (*The Killing Dance*).

Her relationship with Richard removes any doubt from Anita's mind that she and domestication don't mix. Cleaning up after the messes his ideals create forces her to become more of a monster.

In *The Killing Dance*, Anita must challenge the lupa of Richard's werewolf pack because he cannot rule them: they don't believe he will kill. He wants the pack to be run in a more humane fashion, but his hesitation to spill blood causes Anita to become more enmeshed with the monsters than with her own humanity. Although Richard does finally kill Marcus, he does not finish the job and kill Raina and Gabriel. At the end of the book, Anita must complete those two kills or die. Once she kills Raina, she is indisputably the lupa of the Thronnos Rokke Clan. And although she doesn't yet know it, killing Gabriel also sets her up to be the leader and protector of the wereleopard pack.

Even after killing Marcus, Richard is still too humane to keep control of his pack. After he is accused of raping one of the women he auditioned for lupa, Anita goes to Myerton, Tennessee, to save him. In the process, she has to kill a large number of the city's vampires. In *Narcissus in Chains*, Anita is forced to become the pack's Bolverk—worker of evil—to do the evil deeds Richard is unable to because of his principles. She executes Jacob, who intended to kill his way to becoming the pack's leader in order to turn it over to Chimera. Richard is unable to do even those evil deeds that would keep him in power and his pack protected.

The more monstrous Anita becomes in order to make up for Richard's quest for a humane and human life, the more she is pushed into the monster world. But while killing is a step away from normalcy, it also brings her closer to the monsters that she protects, where she discovers a different kind of love, a different kind of intimacy, and a different kind of home.

Anita's Keeping a List, Checking It Twice

> "You can't save everyone," Sylvie said.
> "Everyone needs a hobby."
>
> —*Burnt Offerings*

If there is anything that Anita lives for, it's protecting innocents from the monsters. Because of her preternatural gifts, because she *can* save innocents, she feels it is her responsibility to do so.

Anita may have inherited this belief from her creator. In the afterword of *The Lunatic Café*, Laurell K. Hamilton writes: "If you don't help protect the innocent, then what good are you? If you don't protect those weaker than you, what good are you?" Hamilton is not asking rhetorical questions. She later answers her questions, and her judgment is blunt: "No damn good at all." So Anita keeps a list of those she would kill for, whether to avenge them or keep them safe.

At first, this list mostly consists of humans. Although she kills Nikolaos and many of her supporters to protect Jean-Claude, given the opportunity she would sooner see him dead: she is afraid of the love she might come to feel for him. He is only on her list because if he is the Master of the City rather than Nikolaos, it will save innocents down the line. She also protects Jean-Claude in *Circus of the Damned*, but again, only because if he is in power rather than Mr. Oliver, the human community will be safer.

In *The Killing Dance*, things change: the number of monsters on her list rapidly overtakes the number of humans. First comes Willie: he is the first vampire Anita considers a friend, partly because she liked him when he was human, and most importantly, because he is one of the weakest vampires in St. Louis. Anita tends to trust those who need protection more quickly than she does those who don't.

She also starts saving the monsters for their sake rather than for the sake of humans. Not all monsters are equally monstrous, she discovers. Not only must she protect humans from the monsters, but she needs to protect the monsters from *worse* monsters. After watching Stephen, the werewolf, get cut up and tortured in order to make a porn film for Raina, Anita realizes humans aren't the only ones who can be victims. She not only puts Stephen on her list, but cuddles with him through the night when he is still afraid, even though she has never slept next to a man until daybreak. For Anita, protecting people is more important than her emotional hang-ups or fears of intimacy.

Any vulnerability at all inspires Anita's need to protect. Divided, the lycanthropic community is weak against such monsters as Chimera, who uses each animal's mistrust of other animals against all of the St. Louis lycanthropes. Anita not only befriends the wererats and protects the werewolves and wereleopards, she also organizes a Lycanthrope Coalition to strengthen the position of all wereanimals. As Jean-Claude points out, "It is getting so that a person cannot insult a monster in St. Louis without answering to you, ma petite" (*Blue Moon*).

While protecting those on her "list" is what gets her into most of her troubles, it's also what brings her closer to the monsters. Every monster she trusts has, at some point, benefitted from Anita's protection. Because it is easier for Anita to trust someone who needs help, protecting someone is often her first step in caring for someone—and sometimes even in loving someone.

Monsters Have Feelings, Too

> "So you invited me to come play because I'm now as much of a sociopath as you are."
>
> "Oh, I'm a much better sociopath," he said. "I'd never let a vampire sink his fangs into my neck. And I wouldn't date the terminally furry."
>
> "Do you date anyone, ever?"
>
> He just smiled that irritating smile that meant he wasn't going to answer. But he did. "Even Death has needs."
>
> Edward dating? That was something I had to see.
>
> *—Obsidian Butterfly*

Until *The Killing Dance*, Anita is convinced that monsters have no feelings. She claims they cannot love. The only thing that cures her prejudice? Empathy. Before she can love the monsters, she must feel what they feel.

When Anita becomes part of a triumvirate with a werewolf and a vampire, she is forced to feel all their emotions. This is not a good thing, at first. She puts Richard in as much of a lose-lose situation as he puts her. When he accepts his beast and kills—as Anita begged him to do—it scares Anita away. The worst of it, however, is not that her lover killed. The worst is that, through the triumvirate, Anita also felt the wolves' desire to feed on flesh. She not only learns that Richard enjoys killing and eating Marcus, she is horrified by the possibility that she, too, would have enjoyed it. She is not ready to accept her own monster, not yet.

The Killing Dance is also a turning point in the way Anita sees Jean-Claude. After a vampire is murdered, Anita is surprised to learn that Jean-Claude is not pleased. She assumed he cared for only the power Robert brought to him, not for Robert himself. He sets her straight: "Then you do not understand me at all, ma petite. He was my companion for over a century. After a century, I would mourn even an enemy's passing. Robert was not my friend, but he was mine. Mine to punish, mine to reward, mine to protect. I have failed him." Anita's false assumptions about him incite an anger so strong in Jean-Claude that it brushes "heat along my skin."

After Anita witnesses Richard's wolf-form tearing a bite out of dead Marcus, she runs straight to the Circus of the Damned and into Jean-Claude's arms. While they have sex, she notices that "emotions flowed over his face." She is even more surprised to feel and see his uncertainty during their love-making.

The forced empathy of the triumvirate starts chipping away at her belief that monsters can't love, but there is still one problem: she believes herself to be a monster, too. Although Anita describes herself as "practical" and "ruthless," she struggles throughout the series with the fear that these are negative qualities and that she is a sociopath. The fact that she can kill so easily and without regret frightens her. She doubts her ability, given her occupation as vampire executioner, to love. Learning that the monsters can love is the first step in winning this battle; learning that *she* can love is the second. While the monsters can teach her that they can love, only a sociopath can teach her that a killer can love.

Edward, whom she often refers to as "Death," is Anita's mentor. She believes him to be the ultimate killer, the ultimate sociopath. Although they are friends, she believes he would kill her in an instant, if needed. They are both executioners, both killers, and Edward taught her almost everything he knows. Anita claims he helped create the woman she is. They are, she believes, two sides of the same coin.

So when she discovers that he has a house and a fiancée, and is helping to look after his fiancée's two children, Anita is shocked. At first she doesn't believe he cares for them: she believes he is using them as a cover. It's not until the end of *Obsidian Butterfly* that she realizes Edward would sacrifice his life to protect the woman's son. Protecting is something Anita always understands; when she discovers he can love and protect, it opens her up to the possibility that killing without regret does not preclude the ability to love.

And just in time. In the very next book, Anita meets her soulmate.

A Marriage of Convenience

> Micah turned his face, looked into my eyes, and I felt something inside me open; some door that I hadn't even known existed swung wide. A wind blew through the door, a wind made of darkness and the stillness of the grave. A wind that held an edge of electric warmth like the rub of fur across bare skin. A wind that tasted of both my men. But I was the center, the thing that could hold both of them inside and not break. Life and death, lust and love. "What are you?" Micah asked, his voice a surprised whisper.
>
> —*Narcissus in Chains*

It is fitting that Anita first meets Micah while in her bed and naked. Her relationship with Micah is instantaneous: Micah's beast calls to her beast. As Anita says, "We were like fishermen. We had our net, all we needed was for the fish to stop fighting us and lay still" (*Narcissus in Chains*). The description works, except it's more like they are the fish who must lay still. Their pairing is instinctive and inevitable, and if they (or really, Anita) will only lay still and accept it, they will snap together like magnets. They are biologically meant for each other: he is leopard king and she is leopard queen. Rafael tells her that her beast has already chosen for her, and Micah explains that they "can't help it," which is, perhaps, the only way Micah so quickly gets past Anita's typical moralizing and reluctance to add another man into her bed.

Micah is different from her other men: Micah is easy. Like most of the men Anita ends up loving, Micah first needs her protection, but that is where the similarities end. Micah admires the traits in her that Richard finds repulsive. He sees Anita's sociopathic tendencies as "practical," because they keep her pard safe, Richard's pack safe, and her friends safe. Where Anita doubts her ruthlessness is a good quality, Micah is so certain it is a positive that he values her for it.

Micah also takes the traditional role of wife in their relationship and home. He keeps the peace. When Anita has trouble growing into her relationship with Nathaniel, it is Micah who forces her to deal with it. He gives her a look that says, "Fix this, or I'll be mad at you, too" (*Incubus Dreams*). And she does, because he is also the one who started one of her most treasured rituals: after Micah discovered that Nathaniel had not read *Peter Pan*, he suggested they all read aloud in bed. If she's running late after a tough night, he and Nathaniel wait up for her.

Perhaps this is why Micah is the first man in her life whose love she makes a concerted effort not to pick at, "to see if it would unravel." But Anita Blake does not trust love, so despite her intentions, she does pick at it. She discovers it does not unravel. It is fitting that, by the end of *Micah*, she uses Micah's blood as a circle of protection: a symbol, perhaps, of her newfound trust in him.

As perfect a wife Micah is to her, he is not even the most important factor in her domestication. She needs another wife: someone she doesn't at first realize she loves, even when everyone else around her does.

Penguins, Spiders, and Leopards, Oh My!

"No, [I'd] kill you to save everybody else you'd destroy."
My voice wasn't soft anymore.
"Even if it destroys you at the same time?"
"Yes."
"Even if it drags our tortured Richard down with us?"
"Yes," I said.
"Even if it cost Damian his life?"
I nodded. "Yes."
"Even if Nathaniel died with us?"
I stopped breathing for a second, and time seemed to do one of those stretches where you have all the time in the world, and none of it. My breath came out shaky, and I had to lick my lips, before I said, "Yes, on one condition."

"And that would be?" he asked.

"That I could guarantee that I wouldn't survive it either."

—*Incubus Dreams*

Nathaniel is the most important factor in Anita's domestication. It is surprising that even after she has the conversation above with Jean-Claude, Anita does not realize that she loves Nathaniel. She is willing to survive the death of everyone she loves, except Nathaniel. How could she not realize that she loves him? As she says, "More than almost any other man in my life, he confused me. Nathaniel was so far outside my comfort zone sometimes that I had no clue" (*The Harlequin*).

It's not just confusion. From the very beginning, she resists the ways of Nathaniel and the other wereleopards. Their comfortable nudity embarrasses her, and their constant touching feels suffocating rather than comforting. They prefer to sleep in puppy piles, with affectionate touches and intertwined limbs to keep them company through the night. When nervous or worried, touch reassures and centers them.

Not for Anita, not at first.

Growing up Catholic with a "Midwestern, middle-class value system" (*Narcissus in Chains*) did not give Anita much comfort with intimacy. She is not at ease with the naked body, partly because it tends to inspire the *ardeur* beyond her control, and partly because of her upbringing. She constantly questions the ethics of her sexual activities. In an interview with Christopher DeRose, Laurell K. Hamilton talked about the creation of the main character for her Merry Gentry series this way: "I wanted someone with an easier attitude about sex. Someone I wouldn't have to argue with all the time the way I do with Anita."

And argue Anita does.

Marianne, her mentor, argues with Anita for four pages in *Blue Moon* before Anita is willing to take the first, simple step toward greater intimacy with her wereleopards—and Marianne asks only that Anita brush Nathaniel's hair. Even this simple gesture raises in Anita a world of worry about her responsibilities to Nathaniel, his submissive sexuality, and her more dominant nature. She fears the consequences of this affectionate act and what it will mean for their relationship.

When Nathaniel almost dies at the end of *Blue Moon*, she is forced into taking a second step towards intimacy in order to save his life. The desire and duty to heal him pushes past her fears and issues with touching his bare skin. She kisses him, her bare breasts against his naked chest.

In fact, much of her sexual growth occurs when she has no choice but to step past her limitations in order to save or protect Nathaniel. These two steps—brushing Nathaniel's hair and touching Nathaniel's naked skin with her own—are the turning points in her relationship with the pard. By *Narcissus in Chains*, Anita becomes more comfortable with the touching and nakedness of the wereleopards, but she cannot enjoy it simply because she enjoys the comfort and warmth of their bodies pressed close to hers at night. She must qualify it, find excuses for it:

> I wake up pressed between Micah and Nathaniel. You can't feed the *ardeur* off of the same person every day, not even a lycanthrope. That's why they used to say that succubi and incubuses killed their victims. You can literally love someone to death. So, I feed on Micah and Nathaniel. Micah as my Nimir-Raj, and Nathaniel as my pomme de sang. No, I'm not having intercourse with Nathaniel. Both of them seem peaceful with the arrangement, though I'm still a little weirded out by it. I'm still hoping the *ardeur* is temporary. (*Narcissus in Chains*)

Anita protects everyone around her, but she never seems to notice the one who most protects her: Nathaniel. Protecting her is something he does without consideration for himself; he is so submissive that he would be happy to die for her. In *Narcissus in Chains*, he offers her the touch that brings her back from Belle's power: "Then Nathaniel was there, and the world was solid again." When Anita almost dies trying to bring Damian, her vampire servant and part of her triumvirate, back from the dead to undo the damage caused by her time away wrestling her moral demons in *Obsidian Butterfly*, it is Nathaniel who offers himself as food for Damian, no matter the risk to his own life. When their triumvirate's power is not fed, it is Nathaniel whose energy is drained to keep Damian's heart beating. When Ulysses is about to kill her, it is Nathaniel who fires the gun that kills Ulysses and saves Anita's life. When Belle Morte attacks her in *Cerulean Sins*, Nathaniel is the one to wrap himself around her and warm her back to normal. Nathaniel is always there for Anita when she needs him.

While the other men in Anita's life may clash, strut their dominance, and test the order of power, Nathaniel rarely complicates her life. He is content to play wife to her and to Micah, to putter in the kitchen and make sure that she eats. He is content to be the submissive one amongst all the dominant and more demanding men in Anita's life; he does not add more posturing to her already complicated love life. She can count on him to always be there when she asks, to always obey her when she needs him, and to always give her support, even if it means giving up his life. The strength he gives her with his submissiveness is given quietly, patiently, and without demand.

It is this quiet and patient approach that ultimately domesticates Anita. Without her realizing it, Nathaniel makes a home for her and Micah. She looks up and there he is, happily puttering in her—his—kitchen. Unlike with Richard, she is not freaked out by this; Nathaniel has earned it. Up until that point, she'd always assumed that when the *ardeur* went away, she would no longer need Nathaniel. She often wondered about getting him an apartment and setting him up with a life of his own.

All the while, he was building a home around her.

Even Jean-Claude acknowledges that it is Nathaniel who can make these little headways into her unease with intimacy and domestication. Of all her men, Nathaniel is the first one to go on an anniversary date and celebrate a special day with her. Jean-Claude sees this and hopes that Nathaniel will make Anita more amenable to anniversaries and expressions of love.

Nathaniel may be the most submissive of all her men, but he is also the most important factor in her domestication. In protecting him, she learns to touch. In being protected by him, she learns to trust him, to be part of a family, and to take and make time for intimacy. His quiet and patient ways domesticate her before she notices, which is possibly the only way she *could* be domesticated.

The Black Wrought-Iron Fence

> I'm happy behind my black wrought-iron fence. The one with the pointy spikes on top. White never really was my color.
>
> —*Danse Macabre*

By *Skin Trade*, Anita is still a monster, still a sociopath, still not white-picket fence material. The difference is, she accepts who she is. She's learned that forgoing the white-picket fence does not mean forgoing the joys and comforts of domestication. Where there is a house with no neighbors to protect innocents from the dangers and monsters in her life, there is also a home with two men she loves. Where there is a succubus needing to feed, there is also true love.

For Anita, finding peace and happiness is not achieved by getting rid of or taming the monster inside her, but by accepting it and allowing herself to love *as* a monster. She is and always will be a wild cat, a predator, a zombie queen. But in opening herself up to that world, she finds a different kind of domestication: one perfect for her.

"Sandwiched between Micah and Nathaniel was the safest, best place I'd ever known" (*Danse Macabre*).

◆　◆　◆

Natasha Fondren is a writer who enjoys a different kind of domestication, too: she lives on the road in a little camper, moving from place to place as her restless spirit calls. Every night, she sleeps in a "puppy pile" with four cats and a husband. Her adventures can be read at natashafondren.com.

This essay sees in the *ardeur* some of what I saw in it eventually, but at first I, like Anita, was pretty horrified. We're both control freaks and the *ardeur* is about losing control. It is the antithesis of all that hard-won refusal and discipline that Anita prided in herself. But without the *ardeur* Anita would still be trapped in herself, in her denials. Without it she'd still be able to hide from herself.

But Devon Ellington also maintains that Anita gives the monsters more help than she gives her human friends. I know that Larry Kirkland vanished from the books when he married and had a child because he's not a shooter. Anita and I are pretty frightened that we'll get him killed. I think that would be too much guilt for Anita to bear. Dolph Storr's about face from calm perfect policeman to near hysterical rage about his son, Darrin, marrying and wanting to become a vampire is still as puzzling to Anita as it is to me. I know he will get past it, but though Anita and Dolph are friends, they are work friends. The same is true of Anita and Zerbrowski. Anita never did, and isn't likely to do, anything with either man; that is just them and being just friends. It's not the same way she was friends with Ronnie Sims.

Ronnie's issues have smashed into Anita's own, and hurt the friendship, but it was Lilth Saintcrow's essay that hit it, I think. Ronnie didn't see Anita as a rival for men because Anita didn't chase them. She was content to let Ronnie hit that. Anita being sexually prolific has thrown Ronnie and made her uncertain how to react. I didn't realize that Ronnie was one of those women who see other women as rivals. When Anita was safe they could be friends, but Anita is no longer "safe." For books neither has been comfortable with their reversed roles. Anita is working on it, and I know Ronnie is, too. I honestly don't know if they will mend their friendship, but the number of men Anita's committed to must take up a lot of her time. Sex with that many men would be okay, but trying to date this many people, does Anita really have time for any other friendships? I didn't do this on purpose, but

I'm pretty sure if I was trying to date, or live with, this many men and still worked the hours Anita and I work that I'd be pretty short on time to go out shopping with the girls, too.

—*Laurell*

Ardeur's Purpose

DEVON ELLINGTON

Series books provide particular challenges, because the writer has to take the reader on an ever-expanding journey. The stakes have to rise, book by book, and the characters need to grow and deepen as the readers do. Well-done series enable authors to develop their characters over a long period of time, allowing them to grow, change, backslide, empower, frustrate.

All too often, this doesn't happen. Many publishers believe that readers want a level of comfort, want to know what they're getting, which underestimates the readers' hunger for challenges met by fascinating characters in astonishing ways. So authors pack their characters' development all into one book, or even three books, and then keep them on fixed paths, simply tossing a challenge du jour their way that doesn't really change them, and that keeps the readers in their own comfort zone.

This is particularly true when it comes to series that feature a romantic relationship. Convention—and many publishing guidelines—insist that, once the protagonist and the "hero" meet, every other serious suitor falls away, and once they kiss or have sex, the *woman* must be monogamous. And so often a series, especially one with a female protagonist, will fall flat after a few books, because the character progressed from A to B and maybe even reached C, but then found "true love"—after which point any challenge becomes a threat to the primary relationship, instead of taking advantage of the challenges presented by the myriad facets of a strong woman's daily life. This isn't the way it works in reality, and it doesn't make for rewarding reading. Treating relationships like living, growing organisms (and not just falling into clichés about temptations and fidelity) means the challenges and conflict must always be growing.

Laurell K. Hamilton's Anita Blake series is exceptional in its commitment to pushing its main character to continue evolving. The fact that Hamilton is able to not only sustain Anita's personal development for so many books, but also keep pushing her boundaries, is unusual. The fact that she does is through sex—through the *ardeur*—is even more unique. Anita is one of the first (and, even now, one of the few) popular human (at least at the start of the series) female characters to maintain multiple relationships and not only *not* be punished for it, but grow and improve because of it.

Guilty Pleasures ends with the words: "I know who and what I am. I am the Executioner, and I don't date vampires. I kill them." Yet by the fifteenth book, *The Harlequin*, Anita's become someone who'll say: "I'll compromise; I'll bend" to make someone she loves happy, in spite of her fear that, in bending, she just might break. It's a huge change for her, almost unfathomable—and the *ardeur*, rather than being just an excuse for sexier books, is the reason for the change.

The *Ardeur*'s Challenge

When Anita develops the *ardeur* in *Narcissus in Chains*, she has only recently resolved the series' previous primary conflict: the choice between Richard and Jean-Claude. This isn't just a matter of deciding which one to have a relationship with, but a decision about what Anita wants for her life. Does she want to strive for normalcy and try to ignore the fact that she is different, the way Richard does? Or does she choose to accept what she is—a powerful necromancer, and a part of the supernatural community? Though she remains tied to Richard through their triumvirate, and at the beginning of *Narcissus in Chains* has made the decision to work on her relationships with both men, it is Jean-Claude with whom she throws in her lot, having taken an important, if uneasy, step toward self-acceptance.

This is where the typical series would consider its work done. But this is where Hamilton uses the *ardeur* to raise the stakes instead.

Despite rejecting Richard's way of reacting to his supernatural situation, Anita has not yet found her own. She accepts her abilities, but she is still not comfortable using them unless she is backed against a wall in a life-or-death situation. We see this at the end of nearly every book, where desperation leads Anita to discover yet another facet of her powers. She ignores her own nature as often and completely as possible.

Learning to accept her abilities isn't Anita's only personal challenge. Due to her size, her looks, and the world being the way it is, she has had to be twice as good to get half the respect from the men with whom she's forced to work. Her intelligence and her strength have allowed her to prove herself, both to herself and others, but to retain the respect she has earned, she cannot show any weakness, and so she has issues with intimacy and control.

Anita lost her mother at an early age and wound up with a stepmother, Judith, who wanted Anita to be more like her other daughter, more in keeping with a traditional definition of femininity—which meant conforming, something Anita was unwilling and in some ways unable to do. Anita was also torn between grandmothers—her mother's mother, who helped hone her natural animation powers, and her father's mother, who believed her powers were evil. Her choice of profession, of accepting her paranormal abilities and using them as a viable skill in the workplace, meant she was, in a way, cast out from her family. Her own church also cast her out for her abilities. And the boy she was engaged to in college rejected her as well. She spent most of her adult life avoiding situations in which she could be hurt. As a result—and likely as a result of her Catholic upbringing as well—she is against casual sex. She is uncomfortable with romantic relationships, especially the idea of relying on someone else emotionally.

Because of all this, the *ardeur* is tailor-made to challenge Anita by pushing her out of her comfort zone. She is forced to have casual sex to survive, but even more, the *ardeur* takes away her self-control and forces her into long-term intimate arrangements—all of which forces her to deal with the very issues she's successfully avoided in her adult life so far. Learning to deal with a consuming kill-or-be-killed lust is just as much of an emotional challenge for her as a physical one.

Anita's Growth

Anita claims to hate the *ardeur*. It robs her of her self-control and, if ignored long enough, her choices. She tries to limit its violation of her sense of morality by choosing men she can care about (Micah, Jason, Nathaniel, Asher, etc.) but still ends up using and hurting people (Requiem, London, Wicked, and Truth, and even, at times, Nathaniel and Jason), which upsets and frustrates her.

But she also *likes* the *ardeur*. She just doesn't want to admit it. While she wants more control over it, she's not willing to give it up. She enjoys the sex. And when the *ardeur* flows, she can let go of the self-control that is her rule in her day-to-day dealings.

Anita drives away (or shoots) anyone who might dominate her in life, but then submits to rough trade and even group sex in front of an audience, as with Auggie in *Danse Macabre*. She tries to make lust transformative by connecting it with love, yet there's the side of her that likes it rough and enjoys the pain. But since it's *ardeur*, well, as Jason points out, she doesn't have to take responsibility. "I thought you were growing, changing, but what you just said blames it all on the *ardeur*. You didn't do any of it. Not your fault. If you fuck everything that moves while under the sway of the *ardeur*, you're still blameless," Jason says in *Incubus Dreams*, and again, in *Blood Noir*: "The *ardeur* is like the perfect excuse to never have to say you're sorry." Even Richard points it out: "You never plan it, Anita. It's weirdly never your fault." She wants all those urges she "shouldn't" want to be *ardeur*. But those urges aren't Belle Morte; they're Anita's good-girl Catholic side exploding from years of repression.

One of the most infuriating aspects of Anita's character is that, when faced with an option that will lessen the effect of the *ardeur*, sometimes something as simple as eating regular meals, she deliberately ignores it.

She could make the choice to train her powers as diligently as she used to train her body, running with Ronnie. But she doesn't.

She's got to be the hero, and yet she refuses, over and over and over again, to take the basic steps to give herself the strength to do what's necessary. She has the ability to tap into her own power at will, but she refuses to do so until those she loves are in danger. Entities attracted by her powers and potential want her to use it, and want to use her for their own ends. She's constantly fighting others' attempts to turn her into an object of power instead of an individual wielding her own power. She wants control of herself and her life, yet time and time again she's passive about the simplest tasks, such as eating a hamburger, letting others push her into life-or-death situations and avoiding the responsibilities that come with power.

What finally pushes Anita to start to take responsibility for her powers, however, is the effect it has on other people. Protecting others—physically, if not emotionally—has always been a key part of Anita's character. Once her triumvirate forms with Damian and Nathaniel, their continued existences depend on her ability to control and feed the *ardeur* and other hungers. It's no longer an option to indulge in her self-destructive tendencies to ignore her own well-being, because now it's not just her own life at stake. She still gets to be the breadwinner—but in more than just financial terms. She supplies the sheer life force that Nathaniel and Damian require for survival. If she ignores or abdicates her responsibilities to them, she will have death on her hands without the safety of a warrant—it will be due to her own selfishness. If she refuses to take responsibility, her extended family will die. It's no longer just about her, her needs, her wants.

This is the other thing the *ardeur* has forced upon her: connections to other people. Anita has spent a great deal of her life alone, but with the *ardeur*—if she wants to retain control over whom she feeds it with—that is no longer an option. In her attempts to transform desires that could take her down a path of enormous destruction into something positive, she has built, in spite of herself, an inter-species family—one founded on guilt and *ardeur*, but one that Anita becomes more and more comfortable with as the series continues. Anita has spent most of her life running from emotional intimacy, and so learning to accept it now is difficult. The only reason the *ardeur* forces her to try is that doing so is less difficult than accepting the idea of casual sex.

The first real steps Anita takes toward this kind of emotional intimacy are with Micah. Micah's value is often pushed to one side in the books, although he frequently displays his compassion, intelligence, and diplomacy along with sexual prowess. Not only does he strengthen as a character worthy of Anita, he holds his own in *Micah,* assisting in her work as an animator and making it one of the better books in the series, both plot- and character-wise. Hamilton uses the book to explore the growing intimacy between them—apart from feeding the needs of *ardeur*—and to highlight the ways Anita is beginning to grow and change as a result.

The intimacy she allows to develop with Micah extends to others she is tied to as well, particularly Jean-Claude (with whom she had been the most intimate previously), Asher, and Nathaniel. She starts to feel responsible for (and to) those she sleeps with, not just physically, but emotionally, too. At the end of *The Harlequin,* she pledges to try to learn how to meet Nathaniel's needs, and in *Blood Noir,* she shows a level of both acceptance and responsibility of her role in the expanded family group, calling both Jean-Claude and Micah to discuss going home with Jason to support him during his family's crisis. She backslides again in *Skin Trade,* sneaking out to join Edward in Las Vegas for a job while Jean-Claude is still (literally) dead to the world and not even calling Micah, but by *Skin Trade* she's also reached a feeling of home: "I'd learned that the *ardeur* could be about friendship and not just romance. . . . It was about that feeling of belonging, of being home."

It's not only her responsibilities to Micah, Jean-Claude, and Nathanial that Anita begins to own up to. Requiem is kidnapped and tortured by Vittorio in *Skin Trade* because he is one of hers—even though he wished to break away. Anita saves him, and though that in itself isn't unusual, it's not done with the same sense of being put-upon she seems to feel in the earlier books. Her lovers are her responsibility, because they can be used against her. That doesn't stop her from using them, but at least, as the books progress, she doesn't resent it quite as much when she has to take action to save them.

Anita also has the power of several different animals within her, each wanting a different mate, each wanting to force her to shape-shift into its form and claim her as its own. She resents these competing forces, and external ones looking to influence the battle, but she also spends many books resenting the weres, who are as helpless about being drawn to her as she is about being drawn to them. By *Skin Trade*, however, when she finds that Domino (who isn't any happier about his attraction to her than she is) feels like "home" to her, she doesn't feel the need to punish him for it, as she would have done had they met earlier in the series. Instead of trying to deny the animals inside her, or cut them out of her life, she's learning to integrate them and starting to search for ways to use them responsibly.

Though she still has a way to go, Anita has experienced a level of growth, thanks to the *ardeur*, that would have been unimaginable at the beginning of the series. Anita has watched how Richard's refusal to accept the dual sides of his nature is destroying him, and it seems that she is learning—from his mistakes as well as her own—to make smarter choices. The question becomes how Anita will resolve this conflict and merge her desires with what she thinks is "right" in future books. Will she come to a more holistic acceptance of herself? Will she stop the acts of self-loathing, like denying herself regular meals and rest, and start enjoying the positive aspects of the life she's building? She starts appreciating both Micah and Nathaniel's roles in her life by *Danse Macabre*. Can she allow herself small moments of contentment, even though her life doesn't fall into the realm of what is considered "normal" by society's monogamous standards? Richard can choose to stay stuck; Anita has chosen not to. The door is now open to the possibility that Anita will be able to see past her own self-inflicted martyrdom and come to terms with the fact she is dealing with unique individuals with unique needs. Every action she takes has consequences. The sooner she faces them, the less of a chance there is for the situation to escalate into something none of them can handle. Hamilton's gift is that she makes us continue to care about Anita on this journey, and her skill in creating Anita's conflicted inner and outer lives makes us hunger to see the outcome. She's created a verbal *ardeur* between the series and the readers.

Other Strong Women

While the *ardeur* has pushed Anita's boundaries in many ways, there are other personal challenges that she has yet to face.

Anita is uneasy with women from the beginning, and it only gets worse as the series progresses. She loses Ronnie, her best friend and staunchest ally, making less and less time for the person who, at the beginning of the series, was central to her life and her sanity. Anita shuts Ronnie out repeatedly, and then is surprised when Ronnie is so angry with her. Not only is she surprised, she finds reasons to justify her shoddy treatment of the woman she claims is her best friend. Anita has no trouble being kind and loving to a vulnerable man, such as Nathaniel, but should a woman, even her supposed best friend, need some understanding, Anita lashes out instead.

Anita has time for Claudia, her wererat bodyguard, but Claudia is under her in the hierarchy. So is Cherry, the wereleopard nurse, and Dr. Lillian, the wererat doctor. Anita isn't comfortable around any women who could be considered her equal, and she usually deals with her discomfort by provoking a fight. She hates Thea, the powerful, manipulative mermaid. She's in immediate conflict with Bibiana, the hugely powerful weretiger queen in *Skin Trade*. Although she manages to save Bibiana and several others when she defeats Vittorio in order to retrieve Requiem, there's a strong sense that it was more because Bibiana happened to be there than because Anita feels any responsibility to the weretiger queen.

Anita has a natural distrust of anyone whose power rivals or surpasses her own—likely in part because that makes them capable of using Anita against her will. And the purveyors of the strongest power in the series are female—especially Belle Morte and Marmee Noir. Whether Anita realizes it or not, it seems that she's building her own line of energy in preparation to take on one or both of these powerful females. However, she is also forced into alliance with one or the other of them almost as often as she needs to defend herself against them. Did the loss of her own mother at a young age and her contentious relationship with her stepmother make it impossible for Anita to trust any woman again? (Both Belle Morte, as the source of Jean-Claude's line, and Marmee Noir, the mother of all vampires, are positioned as mothers in the series.) Or will Anita learn to meld her power with that of another female character further down the series in order to benefit both?

Human Friendships

Friendship is another area in which Anita does not excel. Jason is Anita's truest friend, in every sense of the word, and one of the few people who can tell her things she doesn't want to hear. Jason manages to get through to her when no one else, not even Micah or Jean-Claude, can. By *Blood Noir*, their relationship has grown to the point where, instead of getting passive aggressive or simply aggressive, as she would have earlier in the series or with one of her other lovers, Anita discusses her anger with Jason at his flirting when she is supposed to be his date with an openness and an honesty she shares with no one else. And they come to a solution that works for both of them, without one or the other feeling shorted. With Jason, Anita achieves a level of honesty and equality on a personal level that she can't seem to achieve with anyone else. But Jason is two other things: her lover (on occasion) and not human.

While Anita has grown by leaps and bounds in her ability to maintain emotionally healthy relationships with werecreatures and vampires, the deeper Anita goes in dealing with the monsters, the less room there is for humans in her world. She'll give the undead second, third, fourth chances—even Gretchen, the vampire who wants her dead because of Gretchen's unrequited love for Jean-Claude. But Anita won't give humans who've shown her loyalty the same slack. Ronnie isn't the only friend Anita loses during the course of the books, and her friends are few and far between to begin with. She doesn't like her coworkers or her manager very much. She loses interest in the young, talented animator she mentors, Larry Kirkland, when he falls for Tammy, a witch who happens to be a cop (another strong woman not to Anita's taste). After that Larry becomes peripheral in her life.

The one human with whom her friendship remains strong is Edward, who happens to be a sociopath assassin and not one of her lovers. With Edward, Hamilton has created one of the most complex, intriguing characters in current literature. He threatens Anita more than once; he'd kill her in an instant if it suited him; and part of him wants them to be pitted against each other to prove, once and for all, who is the best killer. Yet when there's a big problem, each relies on the other as an extension of him- or herself. Edward, who planned to torture the location of the Master of the City out of Anita in *Guilty Pleasures*, instead helps treat her vampire bites with holy water and joins her invasion of Nikolaos's lair. When Anita travels to New Mexico to help in *Obsidian Butterfly*, she is the one he trusts will get his family to safety if he doesn't survive.

Like Anita, Edward has also grown during the course of the series. For one thing, he is now capable of love: He loves his fiancée and his step-children. His respect and friendship for Anita and his understanding of her have grown into a type of love. Anita believes that they've reached a point where Edward might not be able to commit the final kill should Anita lose all of herself into monstrous power: "Because I now know that even [Edward] would hesitate. He loved me too much" (*Skin Trade*).

Their friendship has actually grown throughout the series. Still, it's not friendship in the traditional sense; its roots are in their shared working life. Though Edward's relationship to the supernatural community is different than Anita's, it shapes his life just as much as Anita's does hers.

Anita isn't always the one who decides to end a friendship. In a shocking character arc, Dolph Storr turns on her for consorting with monsters, showing a rabid prejudice that is astonishing in a man who, book after book, demonstrated so much level-headed cop sense. Anita often wonders why Dolph was placed on the squad, whether it was punishment for something: "Dolph had pissed somebody off, or he wouldn't have been here. But Dolph, being Dolph, was determined to do the best job he could. He was like a force of nature. He didn't yell, he was just there, and things got done because of it" (*Guilty Pleasures*). That makes it all the more disturbing when, in later books, he loses his temper on more than one occasion with Anita: "Dolph trashed the room. . . . He finally picked one chair up and seemed to take a special grievance against it. He smashed the metal chair into the floor, over and over" (*Cerulean Sins*). (The explanation that his son is marrying a vampire who wants to turn him isn't enough to make this transformation believable. There's got to be more to it. Perhaps somewhere, before Anita met him, he demonstrated prejudice against a particular group, and that's what landed him on this squad.)

Dolph starts to lose trust in Anita in the seventh book, *Burnt Offerings*, because she's dating Jean-Claude: "I don't think anything short of giving up Jean-Claude would have satisfied Dolph. I wasn't sure that was an option anymore for a lot of reasons." By *Narcissus in Chains*, Dolph loathes her for the choices she has made in her personal life. "How can you fuck a corpse?" he asks, and later in the same book, when he asks if she's sleeping with Micah and she admits it, "He stood trembling in front of me, big hands in fists at his side, and for just a second, I thought he might do something, something violent, something we'd both regret. . . . Whether Dolph cried or not, it was his business, not mine."

It seems unfair that while she rescues Nathaniel, whom she's never even met, from Zane in *Burnt Offerings*, she won't make it her business to comfort a human she claims is a friend. Does her growing understanding of the complexities in the preternatural community preclude her ability to maintain human relationships on any level? Why can't she grow in her human-based relationships as well as her para-human ones? Is Hamilton giving Anita room to grow in her dealing with humans, or taking her down a path that will exclude them as anything but civilians serving as collateral damage in power wars? At this point in the series, it's not yet clear.

The Future: Asher as Redemption

While Anita has grown from the *ardeur*, and learned much more control over it, neither it nor her other growing powers are done with her yet. And it's a vampire who holds the most hope that Anita can and will use those powers for something positive and ultimately beautiful, who travels down some of the more complex corridors of the *ardeur* with her and holds a ray of hope and light in her bleak and ever-darkening world, even though he possesses an element of danger. It's not Jean-Claude. It's Asher.

Half of him is beautiful, half of him is scarred. Jean-Claude still loves him, and although Anita first sees Asher through Jean-Claude's memories (courtesy of the triumvirate), she soon learns to love Asher for who he is. She doesn't simply desire him; she loves him: "It was Asher, and I loved him" (*Skin Trade*).

He first appears in *Burnt Offerings*, a tool belonging to the Vampire Council, given the opportunity to exact revenge on Jean-Claude. He's full of self-loathing, yet Anita can see him for what he was and is: "I looked at him and he was beautiful." His response to her is, "What I saw in your face, no one else can give me." Asher steps back, no longer the Council's weapon. It is the first gift she gives him, and one of the times in the series when she is genuinely selfless.

In *Cerulean Sins*, Anita offers Asher a place in her bed with Jean-Claude, both to protect him from being taken back to Belle Morte via Musette and because of her growing feelings for him. Asher warns her that if she takes him to her bed and then rejects him, he will leave anyway, as the pain will be too much to bear. She swears she won't, they all go to bed, and of course, she breaks her promise. She refuses to follow through and take responsibility for the effect her actions have on those around her, the same way she does with Requiem, London, Wicked, and Truth. She refuses to let Asher walk out of her life because *she* doesn't want it, and yet she refuses to give him what he needs, even when he's honest with her from the beginning.

Belle Morte tries to bind Asher to her again, which nearly kills him, but because Anita breaks another of her own rules and lets Asher feed from her, she and Jean-Claude are able to save him. Later, in *Danse Macabre*, when they have sex and he feeds off her, he nearly kills her. "He fed on my neck, and as long as he fed, the orgasms continued . . . It was one of the things that made him so dangerous. While you were in the middle of all that pleasure, you could forget . . . I lay there like a broken doll." Despite the danger, Anita is not willing to give Asher up. "I'm not afraid because you almost killed me. I'm afraid because you almost killed me, and I still want to touch you."

Feeding the *ardeur* with Asher gives him back his autonomy. What she refused to give him in *Cerulean Sins*, she gives him in *Danse Macabre*:

> "It was not blood that brought my power, Anita. It was you, you wanting me more than anyone else. . . . I could see into your heart, and I saw only me there."
>
> "Yes," I said, "otherwise I'd have been wicked pissed about the whole almost-killing-me thing."

Asher is the one who helps her turn the corner with her *ardeur*, showing her it can be used with positive results instead of treating it as something to be ignored until it can't be anymore, then satiating it, then ignoring it again, etc., in a downward spiral. Asher is proof that there's a choice, that the spiral has potential to move upward.

Anita questions her choices. She feels that no matter how hard she works, how many bad guys she kills, and what she does for the police and the people she loves, that the bad comes in faster than it can be cleared away.

And yet, Asher is proof that there's hope in what she is and what she does. Asher's presence and character arc indicate the possibility that there's a reason Anita's powers continue to grow, and that the end doesn't have to be destruction.

As Jean-Claude points out in *Skin Trade*: "Everyone believes that Belle Morte's line is weak because our power is love, but really, ma petite, what is more powerful than love?"

◆ ◆ ◆

Devon Ellington publishes under a half a dozen names in both fiction and non-fiction, including the paranormal Jain Lazarus Adventures and (as Cerridwen Iris Shea) the Merry's Dalliance pirate tales. Her blog on the writing life is Ink in My Coffee: http://devonellington.wordpress.com.

I know Melissa, Mel, and I know her background in the law. I found her area of expertise applied to my series to be interesting, but not surprising. What the United States of America has done to the legal vampire citizens in my world is one of the worst abuses of personal freedom that I could imagine. You are a legal citizen, you pay taxes, but still don't have the right to vote. Worse, you can be killed by a court order of execution because you've been deemed too dangerous to be held for trial.

Now, I mention in the early books some incidents that caused this change. There was a master vampire who escaped a maximum security prison by using mind tricks, and he slaughtered a lot of people getting out. He killed more when he got to the outside. I used the headlines of murderers and rapists who are paroled early and then go on to commit more and often worse crimes. What if these people had superhuman strength, mystical powers, and were almost unstoppable? Would we as a society tolerate the slaughter, or would we fight back with the scariest, and best, weapon we have, the law? I took the worstcase scenario view and gave us legal executioners with the full weight of the law and courts behind them.

Mel points out, rightly, that the judicial branch is almost gutted in this process except that it signs off on warrants of execution. But one thing she fails to add is that Anita and the other executioners don't just kill vampires. They kill wereanimals, human beings when they're not furry. It takes more evidence to get a warrant of execution on a wereanimal than a vampire, but in some Western states if you shoot someone dead and later a blood test proves that the human body was a lycanthrope you get off scot-free, because the law assumes that simply by being a wereanimal the person was a real and present threat to your safety, and shooting him or her was a sort of weird self-defense.

The vampires and their lobby are fighting to get representation to go with the taxes they're paying. But all the preternatural citizens of the United States are in jeopardy from the very forces that protect the rest of us. It is a civil rights nightmare, and that part, at least, I did on purpose. But in researching the law, I lost some illusions. I thought the law was supposed to be about justice, but it is not. The law is about the law, and it can only be interpreted and administered as it is written. A badly written law can tie the hands of a good judge because he, or she, has no room to do what they feel is right, because they are charged with upholding the letter of the law, not always the spirit of it. I am a great deal more cynical about the legal system than I was when I wrote the first Anita book, and a great deal more respectful of the nearly impossible task of writing laws that are fair and protect us all equally.

In the end equality is something the law strives for, but it's almost impossible to achieve. In my world we've given up the pretense of fairness for vampires and shapeshifters. I explored how much Anita's attitude has changed in *Skin Trade*, where she realizes the law doesn't have enough room for some of the things she knows to be true about vampires. Weak ones can be controlled by the powerful and they can be as innocent as any bespelled human, so why should they die as if they're the big, bad vampire? In *Skin Trade* Anita actually saves more people than she kills. I think it may be a first.

—*Laurell*

Trying the System

MELISSA L. TATUM

In Anita Blake's world, the monster lurking in the dark has emerged from the closet and become the monster who lives next door. College students earn degrees in preternatural biology, cops must determine whether the corpse at their murder scene will come back to bite them (literally!), and EMTs must treat everything from humans to vampires to shifters to all sorts of other formerly mythical creatures. And the criminal justice system struggles with how to handle beings with superhuman strength and abilities. How do you incarcerate a vampire who can bend the bars of the cell and escape? How do you impose pretrial detention on a vampire who can exert mind control powers on his jailer, compelling the jailer to open the cell and forget ever doing so?

Over the first dozen books in the Anita Blake series, the U.S. government wrestles with these issues, and while it laudably decided to make vampires legal citizens of the United States, it unfortunately decides to flagrantly violate approximately one-half of their constitutional rights by imbuing federal marshals with the legal authority to be vampire executioners. No search warrants or arrest warrants for vampires; instead, courts issue warrants of execution, essentially creating a system where the sniper and the cop combine to create an assassin with a badge and give a whole new meaning to the phrase "execute the warrant."

To fully understand what is happening in Anita's universe, we must take a brief detour through the somewhat convoluted thicket of the criminal justice system. The American criminal justice system prides itself on being a model of fairness, a system founded on the bedrock principle that it is better for ten guilty men to go free than for one innocent person to be convicted. The system achieves this goal by creating an elaborate set of procedural protections, and the most important of those procedures are articulated in the U.S. Constitution. Twenty-five clauses in the first ten constitutional amendments address individual rights and create boundaries to prevent the government from overreaching. Over half of these clauses, fourteen of the twenty-five to be exact, deal with the criminal justice system. Clearly, the Founding Fathers thought it important to spend a significant portion of our primary governing document outlining the key working principles of the criminal justice system.

These principles govern everything from police investigations and interrogations and arrests to the trial and sentencing process. They also provide endless fodder for books, movies, and television shows. Americans are addicted to legal thrillers in every form, from John Grisham's *The Firm* to the Law & Order franchise to *Legally Blonde*. The legal process also provides a microcosm for books and movies and television shows to explore how society interacts with those who challenge its norms—think *To Kill a Mockingbird*, *Minority Report*, or *X-Men*.

In addition, these principles provide endless fodder for politicians and the media who seek to manipulate public reaction. Every time the specter of Willie Horton is dragged into the spotlight, every time some media pundit pontificates about the killer who went free on a legal technicality, the public condemns the legal system for placing the rights of murderers above the rights of their victims. What the politicians and the media gloss over is that these principles are not legal technicalities; rather, they are rights. When our Founding Fathers wrote the U.S. Constitution, their purpose was to design a system that protected each person's liberty by ensuring that the government must justify any decision to deprive a citizen of that most cherished right—freedom. The Declaration of Independence speaks of life, liberty, and the pursuit of happiness as the inalienable rights of all men; the Constitution proclaims that it intends "to secure the Blessings of Liberty to ourselves and our Posterity."

At the same time, the Founding Fathers understood that it is part of human nature for the group to join together against those individuals who do not conform to group norms. Humans naturally clump together in everything from high school cliques to the Kiwanis club. And they have words, often negative, to describe those who don't—nonconformist, loner, someone who marches to the beat of a different drum. In recognition of these tendencies, the Founding Fathers created a criminal justice system that is a study in contrasts, a balance between group and individual rights.

On the one hand, the entire purpose of the system is to protect society as a collective from the aberrant behavior of certain individuals: a criminal case is always the *State v.* or the *People v.* the individual defendant. Every society establishes behavioral norms—rules that define what conduct is acceptable and what is not. Not all "unacceptable" behavior is criminal; rather, each society must define for itself what behavior it will treat as "criminal," as so unacceptable that individuals who violate those norms must be singled out for punitive sanctions. It's the difference between littering and wearing white shoes after Labor Day; they are both aesthetically displeasing, but only one is a crime.

On the other hand, the whole purpose of the criminal trial is to protect the individual from society. Society can protect itself from aberrant behavior by imposing criminal sanctions on individuals, but only if it follows the proper procedures. The United States is a system of checks and balances—three branches of government balancing each other and ensuring the Constitution is obeyed. In the criminal justice system, the executive branch, through the police and the prosecutor's office, investigates crime and instigates the process of seeking criminal sanctions. Indeed, this division of labor is at the heart of the successful *Law & Order* television show, now in its record twentieth season. Roughly the first half of each episode follows the police investigation, while the second half focuses on the prosecution.

The police and prosecutors, however, are just two aspects of the system. Presiding over both of them is the judicial branch, which, through the trial and appellate process, ensures that the police and prosecutors do not overstep their boundaries. Much of the dramatic tension in the second half of *Law & Order* arises from the rulings of the judges. Will the confession be suppressed? Will the plea bargain be accepted? Will the surprise witness be allowed? In answering these questions, the judicial branch refers to and relies upon the Constitution, thereby administering a fair process that protects the individual rights of defendants.

In Anita Blake's world, the process has become skewed, at least with respect to vampires. The role of the judicial branch is minimal; it exists only to review and issue warrants of execution. Issuing a warrant is usually the beginning of the court's involvement in a criminal case, not the beginning *and* the end. With no trial and no jury, the role of the judicial branch is all but eliminated, leaving the mission of protecting the public from criminal vampires squarely and heavily on the shoulders of the executive branch. Indeed, in *Incubus Dreams*, one cop challenges Anita's actions, asking, "[W]ho made you judge, jury, and [executioner]?" To which Anita replies, "The federal and state government."

The decision to essentially eliminate the role of the judicial branch is deeply troubling, because in the American system, "guilty" and "deserving of punishment" are not necessarily the same thing. A defendant may have "done the deed" but offers an acceptable excuse, such as self-defense. While we don't condone killing another human being, we also don't believe you have to sacrifice yourself—it is okay to defend yourself, even if the result is that you kill your attacker. Sorting out these types of claims is part of the judicial branch's job.

The American system also believes in tempering justice with mercy tailored to each defendant's personal circumstances. We may not accept a proffered excuse—like acting in the "heat of passion" or "temporary insanity"—as a reason to acquit, but it may be used to mitigate the punishment. While we don't want to encourage people to kill adulterous spouses, we do understand that unexpectedly finding your husband in bed with your sister can cause a person to lose control in a manner that is not likely to happen again—especially if said husband is now six feet under.

These defenses are some of the ways the judicial branch keeps a careful watch on the rights of the defendant and reins in potentially overzealous prosecutors. Our society has decided that why a person commits a crime is relevant to whether and how they will be punished. But these defenses are not available to vampires accused of crimes in Anita Blake's world. The criminal justice system for vampires consists of a stake through the heart and maybe a separation of head from shoulders. (As Anita puts it in *Incubus Dreams*, "dead is at least half their brains spilled, and daylight through their chests.") The why behind their actions is irrelevant.

Examining motivation is only one purpose of the criminal trial. Another purpose, perhaps the primary one, is to put the prosecution's evidence to the test—to put witnesses under oath when they provide testimony and to allow the defense to cross-examine witnesses and present its own evidence. Anita recognizes and wrestles with her conscience on this issue in *Incubus Dreams*; to get a death warrant, "All we needed was proof, or, depending on the judge, strong suspicion. Once I'd been okay with that. Now, it bothered me." In fact, in *Incubus Dreams* Anita actually takes the time to investigate whether the warrant was issued for the correct vampire and, upon discovering it was not, locates and executes the guilty one instead.

In another scene from the same book, Anita explains to the reader why the law was changed to require more than one count of using vampire wiles to have sex before a death warrant could be issued: "Those of us in the middle just didn't like the idea of a death warrant being issued on the say-so of one date who woke up the next morning with a bad case of buyer's remorse." If warrants are being issued for the wrong vampire and other warrants rest solely on one person's say-so, particularly a person with a motive to lie, the process is certainly flawed.

In short, most of the normal procedural protections have been tossed out the window for vampires. The process is clearly skewed.

However, a skewed process is not necessarily also an unconstitutional process. Because vampires are citizens in Anita Blake's world, they are entitled to the same due process and equal protection as all other citizens. For a country founded on the rights of the individual, the United States' history is full of instances where people were categorized by and punished for what they looked like, where they were from, or who they worshipped. We enslaved African Americans, confined American Indians to reservations, incarcerated Japanese Americans, discriminated against Mexicans, and demonized Muslims. In recognition of this basic human impulse, the Founding Fathers inscribed restrictions in the Constitution designed to limit the government's ability to make and enforce laws based on group identity. The government is allowed to make such laws—after all, the September 11 hijackers were all Middle Eastern—but those laws will be strictly scrutinized by the courts, who will require that the government present a compelling case to justify the legal discrimination.

Thus, "due process" and "equal protection" do not mean that everyone must be treated the same. At their most fundamental level, they mean the defendant must receive a fair hearing and any differences in treatment must be justified. What constitutes a fair trial for the average defendant would not be a fair trial for a defendant who possesses superhuman strength and the psychic ability to influence witnesses and jurors. What, then, constitutes a fair trial for a vampire? How do we deal with the "different," the "strange," and the "uncontrollable"?

Although the rights enunciated in the Constitution can be a bit amorphous, they still serve as the touchstone or starting point for answering those questions. In Anita Blake's world, vampires are the "other," the group that challenges the majority's view of itself. They are different and therefore feared and sometimes hated; vampires are almost literally the embodiment of the boogeyman, our childhood fear come to life.

And as with all minority groups, while one segment of the general populace argues for greater understanding, another segment argues that society must enact a slew of laws to protect itself. We saw this in the aftermath of September 11 with the PATRIOT Act and with the cyclical tightening and loosening of immigration and border control laws. Above all, the U.S. Constitution and its individual rights protections exist to control and moderate these impulses. So did Anita's federal government violate the Constitution in authorizing warrants of execution and deputizing vampire executioners? Or do the differences between humans and vampires justify such radically different procedures for handling vampires accused of crimes?

As Felix Cohen, a specialist in American Indian law, declared:

> Like the miner's canary, the Indian marks the shifts from fresh air to poison gas in our political atmosphere; and our treatment of Indians, even more than our treatment of other minorities, reflects the rise and fall in our democratic faith.

Substitute "vampire" for "Indian," and you encapsulate the issue. Granting legal citizenship to vampires means the rules apply to vampires the same as to all Americans. It also means that the same restrictions apply to the government; the government may not violate the rights of vampires any more than it may violate the rights of any citizen. To do otherwise, to create a second and distinct set of rules for vampires, demonstrates a lack of faith in the system and a lack of trust in the system's ability to handle minority groups.

While many people would likely argue that vampires are not "disadvantaged" in the traditional sense (in addition to being powerful and immortal, all but the youngest vampires inhabiting Anita's universe possess some ability that might allow them to thwart or skew the criminal justice process), there is no doubt that vampires are a "disfavored" group. One has only to look at Dolph's reactions to his human son's romantic relationship with a vampire to recognize that prejudice is alive and well in Anita's world. Dolph's hatred is extreme, but his feelings are mirrored in varying degrees by other characters in the series—including, at least in the earlier books, Anita herself.

Anita Blake's world is reeling from vampires being made legal citizens in the U.S. and is struggling to come to grips with what that means. It is precisely in such times of crisis that the Constitution's protections are the most valuable and the most necessary. It is precisely in such situations that the Constitution's protections ensure that our system remains fair and even-handed and does not become twisted by public fear and hysteria. We can't sacrifice the Constitution for expediency. Only if there are no other ways of containing rogue vampires can we justify summary execution.

The critical question is whether the superhuman abilities possessed by vampires justify the government's decision to eliminate the trial process for vampires. While it is true that Anita Blake's world still requires individualized warrants of execution for vampires, so some proof of wrongdoing must be presented, the government has sacrificed the defendant's other rights on the altar of protecting society. Vampire defendants have no ability to respond to the charges, to present witnesses in their own defense, to question the government's witnesses, or to have a jury decide their guilt or innocence.

Even a cursory review reveals a variety of other possible methods of handling vampires suspected of crimes, and while those alternate methods may ultimately prove unsuccessful, the government is morally and legally required to at least give them a try. The police could create and recruit a special squad of vampire officers to handle cases involving vampires, or at least to capture those vampires accused of crimes. The courts could recruit persons with special abilities to sense whether vampires are using their psychic abilities to unduly influence witnesses, jurors, the judge, or anyone else in the courtroom. Perhaps some form of technology could be developed to disrupt the use of those abilities in the courtroom. And those are just a start—clearly, many other options exist.

Society certainly has the right to protect itself, but the federal licensure of vampire executioners is a stunning departure from the checks and balances that form the cornerstone of the American government. And it is a stunning concentration of power in the hands of one individual, something history has taught us is a recipe for disaster. Too much depends on the ethics and integrity of that one person, or at the very least the public's perception of that person's ethics and integrity. It is not enough for a person to *do* right; they must be *perceived* as doing right.

When Anita's government created the special federal marshal position, it gave badges to all vampire executioners with sufficient years of experience and firearm skills. That's a problem. "For some of us it was more like giving a badge to a bunch of bounty hunters with license to kill," explains Anita in *Blood Noir*. Anita also discloses in *Incubus Dreams* that some of those newly minted federal marshals use their badge and the carte blanche provided by the death warrants to justify torture.

Our democratic system ultimately rests on the public's trust of those in power, a trust that the Constitution purchased by setting up a system premised on the idea that although individual segments of the government may be untrustworthy, the three branches possess sufficient checks and balances on each other to keep each separate branch on the straight and narrow. In Anita's words in *The Harlequin*, "When the police go bad, they aren't the police anymore. . . . [They are] criminals"—and the Constitution expects them to be arrested and treated as such. The Constitution's regulations governing the criminal justice system are designed to keep the general public from losing faith in the police and the prosecutors. Individual officers may go bad, but the police department and the district attorney's office as collective entities will remain worthy of the public's trust.

In *The Harlequin*, Malcolm confronts Anita about her decision in *Incubus Dreams* to carry out a warrant by invading his church and executing one of his parishioners. He makes the point that there are no warrants of execution for humans:

> ANITA: The death penalty still exists, Malcolm.
> MALCOLM: After a trial, and years of appeals, if you are human.
> ANITA: What do you want from me, Malcolm?
> MALCOLM: I want justice.
> ANITA: The law isn't about justice, Malcolm. It's about the law.

An insightful, if disturbing, statement. The foundation of the law, the Constitution, declares that the best method of achieving justice is to follow the procedures established in that document. No law enacted in violation of those foundation principles, even one purporting to do justice, can truly be law. No law enacted in violation of those foundation principles should be respected or followed. Officials have a duty to ask whether the laws they are charged with enforcing are in compliance with the Constitution. Even the military, the ultimate bastion of unquestioning obedience, requires its soldiers to recognize and refuse to follow an illegal order. Ask Lieutenant William Calley about My Lai or Adolf Eichmann about the Holocaust; both learned that "just following orders" was not an acceptable defense.

Just following orders is also not an acceptable argument for Anita Blake, federally licensed vampire executioner. Every time Anita executes a warrant (and a thus a vampire), she violates the Constitution. Without legal sanction, an execution is nothing more than murder. The public's faith in the government depends on the government complying with the Constitution and its individual rights protections. The Constitution itself allows the government to tweak the rules, to adapt the contours of the Constitutional guarantees, but the government is not entitled to disregard them all together. And that's what Anita's government did when it licensed vampire executioners.

Anita herself has a fundamental sense of right and wrong. Indeed, much of the conflict in the series derives from Anita's struggles with her own moral code, with the recognition not only that shades of gray exist, but that there may be many more of them than she is comfortable admitting. But while Anita does rely on her own internal sense of justice, she also relies on the guiding hand of the law, and she takes refuge in the protections of the legal system.

Anita recognizes the dilemma licensed vampire executioners pose, even if she shies away from examining it too closely. In *The Harlequin*, Anita gives us some insight into her discomfort:

> I'd been grandfathered in like most of the vampire executioners. . . . The idea was making us federal marshals was the quickest way to grant us the ability to cross state lines and to control us more. Crossing state lines and having a badge was great; I wasn't sure how controlled we were.

Anita is also clearly uncomfortable with the power placed in her hands:

> ANITA: I cleared Avery. Legally, I didn't have to.
> MALCOLM: No, you could have shot him dead, found out your mistake later and suffered nothing under the law.
> ANITA: I did not write this law, Malcolm, I just carry it out.
> MALCOLM: And that justifies slaughtering us?

Anita doesn't respond, but does reveal her internal struggle to the reader:

> I was going to leave this argument alone because I'd begun
> to not like that part of my job. I didn't think vampires
> were monsters anymore; it made killing them harder. And
> it made executing them when they couldn't fight back
> monstrous, with me as the monster.

In a sense, a parallel exists between law enforcement efforts to capture and contain a serial killer and efforts to capture and contain vampires. As with a serial killer, the consequences of failing to capture and contain a criminal vampire are extremely serious; indeed, people will die. But the consequences of violating the Constitution are worse. The system *must* remain intact. To repeat Anita's words, "The law isn't about justice . . . it's about the law." The U.S. Constitution is the supreme law of the land. Tossing out the entire trial process for vampires accused of crimes is an effort to "do justice" at the expense of the law. And that is exactly the type of "justice" the Constitution seeks to curtail. The Founding Fathers firmly believed that true justice is achieved only when the law prevails. They inscribed procedures in the Constitution as part of a deliberate attempt to check those who would act in the name of justice; the procedures reflect a deliberate lack of trust in the judgment of any one person. Before a citizen can be deprived of his or her liberty, several people must pass judgment, and the defendant has a right to be heard and to refute the charges. Vampires are legal citizens in Anita's world, and killing one is the ultimate deprivation of liberty. Summary executions, in the name of protecting society, are the ultimate violation of the Constitution, the bulwark standing between an accused and a mob of vigilantes.

The job of vampire executioner turns the entire U.S. criminal justice system on its head. It tosses out law in an effort to replace it with justice and restricts the number of people who have a say in defining what constitutes justice. It tries the system, finds it wanting, and abandons it altogether for vampires. And the thought of a United States without its criminal justice system scares me. Even more than vampires.

◆   ◆   ◆

Melissa L. Tatum is the Associate Director of the Indigenous Peoples Law and Policy Program at the University of Arizona's James E. Rogers College of Law. Much of her teaching and scholarship focuses on the intersection of minority groups, individual rights, and the criminal justice system. She is also the author of several short stories published by Yard Dog Press.

The vampire as a racial metaphor has been something people have traced in my books from the beginning, but it was not on purpose from my point of view. The vampire represents the other, but that is a lot more than just race. As a Wiccan I can tell you that religion divides you from the mainstream, and will make people look at you as very other. I wasn't Wiccan at the beginning of the series though, so that wasn't what I was thinking at the time.

One of the things Mikhail Lyubansky puts at my door is the lack of non-white characters in my books. Since I get a lot of Hispanic fans loving the fact that Anita is half-Hispanic, I could argue that, but that she looks white seems to be his point. That I can't argue with. I find it interesting that he leaves out Jamil, who is African American and one of the main dominants of the local werewolf pack, and Shang-Da, who is Chinese, the other main bodyguard and dominant. Would he argue that they are subservient to their Ulfric, their Wolf King Richard? Maybe, but that he leaves them out entirely is interesting. One thing I decided early on but have never had on stage was that just as the gene that gives you sickle cell anemia, which is more prevalent in the African American population, turns out to also help fight malaria, I'd decided that it would be cool if it also meant people with sickle cell couldn't "catch" vampirism. It is a cool idea, but I've never managed to get it on stage.

I have debated on whether to share the real reason that there are not more African American or dark-skinned vampires in my books. I can't decide if it's politically correct to say it here. The truth is that all vampires are paler as vampires than they were as live people, thus someone of African American descent would be paler. But how pale? I was pretty sure that if I had characters that were African American but paled them all out that I'd be accused of trying to literally white-wash them. Was I over-thinking it? Maybe, but at the beginning of the series I was very aware that I was white bread as far as I knew, and didn't have any experience here to draw on. I was in my early twenties and I just couldn't figure out a way to ask the question of someone without sounding stupid, or racist, or both. I'm actually planning to grab that particular politically correct dilemma by the horns soon, but because of my own uncertainty early in the series we have a shortage of non-white vampires.

—*Laurell*

Are the Fangs Real?

Vampires as Racial Metaphor in the Anita Blake Novels

MIKHAIL LYUBANSKY, Ph.D.

T hey're physically powerful and capable of unusual speed. They're sexually seductive, in a forbidden sort of way, and dangerous—even the well-mannered, law-abiding ones are, at their core, perilous. They may look human, but they're not. They're monsters, ever ready to prey and feed on human fears, if not their lives. Vampires? Of course. But vampires have never been *just* vampires. As vampire literature expert Elizabeth Miller[1] points out, "the vampire always embodies the contemporary threat." Sure, the Anita Blake novels can be read as light, escapist fiction, but intended or not, the vampires within represent a number of marginalized groups that are perceived as a threat by mainstream society, particularly immigrants and racial minorities. This essay brings this racial metaphor to the foreground.

It All Starts with Dracula

It doesn't, of course,[2] but Dracula is the most famous vampire of all. More than 200 films have been made featuring the Count, and the

---

[1] As quoted in S. Rupp's "The Boy's Got Bite: Why people are vamping it up again, a century after 'Dracula.'"

[2] Before Bram Stoker's 1897 *Dracula*, there was Sheridan Le Fanu's lesbian vampire in

estimate of films that reference Dracula is in the 600s. And that's just film. The Anita Blake series is part of an entire genre of vampire novels (all undoubtedly influenced by Dracula) that now numbers more than a thousand. Perhaps not quite the way the good Count intended, but Dracula did indeed sire an entire universe.

Stoker's novel was itself part of a literary movement called "invasion literature," a genre that included more than 400 books, many bestsellers, in the period from 1871 to 1914. Invasion literature was driven by anxiety about hypothetical invasions by foreigners (H. G. Wells' *War of the Worlds* is the prototypical and best known work), an anxiety that Stoker deliberately (pardon the pun) stoked with his tale of Dracula, who polluted the English bloodline both literally and metaphorically. Indeed, what distinguished Dracula from his vampire predecessors is that his attacks involved not only the possibility of death but the actual loss of one's identity, in particular one's racial identity. As John Stevenson observed in "A Vampire in the Mirror: The Sexuality of Dracula," blood is not just food, semen, and a means to eternal life, but also a "crucial metaphor" for racial identity. Dracula's threat, Stevenson argues, is not mere miscegenation (the mixing of blood) but deracination, for Dracula's sexual partners become pure vampires, with loyalties to Dracula, not Britain.

This perceived racial threat to Britain is the subject of Stephen Arata's "The Occidental Tourist: Dracula and the Anxiety of Reverse Colonization," in which he describes vampirism as "a colonization of the body" and "the biological and political annihilation of the weaker race by the stronger." At a time when British global influence was waning, unrest in its colonies rising, and concerns about the morality of imperialism increasing, Dracula, according to Arata, represented

---

Carmilla (1872), who combined terror with eros, and before that, James Rymer's *Varney the Vampire* (1847), which first introduced many of the standard vampire conventions, including fangs (which leave two puncture wounds in the neck), superhuman strength, and hypnotic powers. Indeed, the modern vampire novel can be traced back as far as 1819, when Lord Byron's physician John Polidori took up Byron's challenge, during a small gathering of friends, to write a ghost story. Polidori's *The Vampyre* was not only the first English-language vampire story but, in the words of cultural scholar Christopher Frayling, also "the first story successfully to fuse the disparate elements of vampirism into a coherent literary genre." It is worth noting that this gathering was also the birth of Mary Shelley's Frankenstein and Byron's own epic poem "Mazappa."

"deep rooted anxieties and fears" of reverse colonization, of civilized Britain "overcome by the forces of barbarism" in the form of immigration from Eastern Europe.[3]

But there was yet another perceived racial menace in nineteenth century England: the Semitic threat. Unlike the "barbaric" East Europeans, at the end of the nineteenth century, European Jews were relatively literate and overrepresented among the bourgeois class. They were nonetheless resented, distrusted, and disliked, perceived as the racial other, an "alien" nation even within their own native England. Dracula embodied this threat, too. As Judith Halberstam observed in *Skin Shows: Gothic Horror and Technology of Monsters*, Dracula "exhibits all the stereotyping of nineteenth-century anti-Semitism" including anti-Semitic physiognomy such as a hooked nose, pointed ears, and claw-like hands, not to mention blood (a measure of racial status and purity) and money, both central features of anti-Semitism. Thus, Dracula is a hybrid of the racial other—the barbaric immigrant from without and the alien Jew within. As such, he posed a double threat to British nationalism and to British women in particular. In Halberstam's words, "he is a monster versatile enough to represent fears about race, nation, and sexuality, a monster who combines in one body fears of the foreign and the perverse."

The American Vampire

By the 1950s, the United States had replaced Britain as a superpower, and the threat of immigration and Semitic hegemony had given way to the racial threat posed by "negroes." Richard Matheson's *I Am Legend*[4] integrates this new political landscape into the vampire

---

[3] As just one example of the novel's overtones of racial threat, consider the Count's taunting comment to Van Helsing and the rest of the vampire hunters at the conclusion of an unsuccessful (from the hunters' perspective) confrontation: "You think to baffle me, you—with your pale faces all in a row, like sheep in a butcher's."

[4] Some readers may be familiar with the 2007 film of the same name, though inexplicably the film replaces the novel's vampires with zombies and depicts Neville as an African American (Will Smith). Film fans may also recall two previous film adaptations of *I Am Legend: The Last Man on Earth* (1964) starring Vincent Price, and *The Omega Man* (1971) starring Charlton Heston. Given the discrepancies between book and film, it is necessary

mythology, with Black Americans, as Kathy Davis Paterson puts it in "Echoes of Dracula," taking on the role of the metaphorical "monstrous Other that threatens the dominant society . . . from within."

The plot of *I Am Legend* consists of a solitary man of English-German stock, Robert Neville, trying to survive in a post-apocalyptic world in which a terrible plague has turned the rest of humanity into vampires. The vampires have no obvious racial markers, but Neville consistently associates them with blackness. For example, he describes the vampires as "something black and of the night" and despairs that "the black bastards had beaten him." But Matheson's use of vampires to discuss race goes far beyond these relatively subtle racial labels. Like Stoker's Dracula, his vampires provide a window into the racial dynamics of the time. Neville's alcohol-induced internal dialogue is telling in this respect and as such is worth a close examination:

> Friends, I come before you to discuss the vampire: a minority element if there ever was one, and there was one.
>
> But to concision: I will sketch out the basis for my thesis . . . . : Vampires are prejudiced against.
>
> The keynote of minority prejudice is this: They are loathed because they are feared. . . .
>
> At one time . . . the vampire's power was great, the fear of him tremendous. He was anathema and still remains anathema.
>
> Society hates him without ration.
>
> But are his needs any more shocking than the needs of other animals and men? Are his deeds more outrageous than the deeds of the parent who drained the spirit from his child? . . .
>
> Really, now, search your soul; lovie—is the vampire so bad? All he does is drink blood.
>
> Why, then, this unkind prejudice, this thoughtless bias? Why cannot the vampire live where he chooses? Why must he seek out hiding places where none can find him out? Why do you wish him destroyed?

---

to note that the analysis in this section is based solely on the book.

> Ah, see, you have turned the poor guileless innocent into a haunted animal. He has no means of support, no measures for proper education, he has not the voting franchise. No wonder he is compelled to seek out a predatory nocturnal existence.
>
> Robert Neville grunted a surly grunt. Sure, sure, he thought, but would you let your sister marry one?

In this relatively brief passage, Matheson quickly establishes the parallel to Blacks (a minority element) and then accurately represents the racial climate of the time period, in which Blacks were "prejudiced against," "loathed because they were feared," and irrationally hated. But Matheson takes the metaphor even further. He notes that the vampires (Blacks) cannot live where they choose (legalized segregation under Jim Crow), must avoid the mainstream community in order to survive (lest a White person make a false accusation), and lack the means to both education and political efficacy. Neville, like many White people of the 1950s, cannot but be aware of the injustice, and there is a part of him that questions its necessity. One gets the sense that he usually keeps such feelings at arm's length, as one must to go along with an unjust system, but on this occasion the whiskey allows him to actually contemplate the system's fairness, to not only recognize the injustice but to attribute the undesirable behavior (a predatory nocturnal existence) of the "minority element" to the injustice of the system rather than to an inherently evil and uncivilized nature. It's a perspective that none of Dracula's hunters could have ever considered and was remarkable even for its day. But it's a fleeting sentiment, one clearly produced by the whiskey, and Neville quickly dismisses it with a question reflecting an anti-miscegenation ideology that was characteristic of both late nineteenth century England and mid-twentieth century United States.

Jean-Claude et al.

The vampires that populate the Anita Blake universe are direct descendants of Dracula and the rest of the vampire lore. This is established in the first book, *Guilty Pleasures*, when we are first introduced to Jean-Claude, who "looked like how a vampire was supposed to look," as well as by occasional references to Dracula himself, as when, in her showdown with the master vampire Nikolaos, Anita remarks, "all we need is the theme from Dracula, Prince of Darkness, and we'll be all set." However, just as the sociopolitical landscape changed significantly from Dracula's time to the time of *I Am Legend*, by the time Anita Blake gets into the vampire hunting business, the sociopolitical Zeitgeist had undergone another substantial shift.

By the early 1990s, the multiculturalism movement had given rise to the possibility that immigration and racial diversity might be valued as well as feared, and mainstream sensibilities had begun to reject explicit racism and xenophobia, even if both often brewed not far below the surface. It is no surprise then that the vampires of the Anita Blake novels have made similarly great strides in this regard since *I Am Legend*, so much so that the Supreme Court's fictional ruling in *Addison v. Clarke* "gave us a revised version of what life was, and what death wasn't" (*Guilty Pleasures*). The upshot of the Court's decision is that vampirism was legalized in the United States, giving vampires legal status along with certain rights. The extent of those rights was still being debated, but *Addison v. Clarke* made the murder of vampires illegal without a court order of execution. Immigration of foreign vampires was still regarded as a threat, but both *Addison v. Clarke* and the vampire suffrage movement signaled a clear growing acceptance of domestic (i.e., American) vampires. As such, Hamilton's vampires may be monsters, but they are no longer aliens.

Not surprisingly, given the sociopolitical changes described above, Hamilton's vampires bear none of the physical markings of their ancestors.[5] They are, however, still a racial threat. They are still feared and distrusted, even hated by many (most?) humans, including at first Anita, who quips in *Guilty Pleasures*, "I don't date vampires. I kill them," a sentiment reminiscent of Neville's previously discussed contempt for human-vampire relationships.

---

[5] This is actually true of most modern vampires (e.g., in the *Buffy*verse and the Twilight series), who don't have hooked noses, pointy ears, clawed hands, or unusual amounts of body hair, as did their ancestors. Even the fangs, the vampire's most recognizable marker, are now discreet, hidden from view and only revealed at the vampire's whim.

The Times, They Are a Changing

What distinguishes the Anita Blake novels from *Dracula* and *I Am Legend* is that Hamilton's novels comprise a long-standing series rather than a single book. At the time of this writing, there are seventeen Anita Blake books, spanning seventeen years. Such a time period allows change, both psychological and political, and Hamilton does not disappoint. The Anita Blake of the later novels is vastly different from the young woman we met in *Guilty Pleasures*.

One of the ways in which Anita changes is that she learns to recognize and value some of the vampires' distinctive characteristics. For example, whereas the vampires' power to heal was mostly an obstacle she had to overcome in the early novels, by *Cerulean Sins* she is able to also see its advantages. "One of my favorite things about hanging out with the monsters is the healing," she says. "Straight humans seemed to get killed on me a lot. Monsters survived. Let's hear it for the monsters."

However, the most telling change in terms of the racial metaphor was in Anita's attitude toward interpersonal relationships with vampires. In *Guilty Pleasures*, she was not only unwilling to entertain the possibility of dating Jean-Claude, she didn't want to have any social relationship with him or any other non-human at all. This early anti-miscegenetic attitude was a product of both dislike and fear, with a little disinterest thrown in. "Did I really believe, what was one more dead vampire?" she asks herself in the opening pages of *Guilty Pleasures*. At that time, her answer to this question is "Maybe." But hate is neither accidental nor coincidental. "We hate most in others what we fear in ourselves," muses Anita in *Narcissus in Chains*. In her case, what she fears is her own monstrosity, her own power and lust. Anti-miscegenation attitudes can be interpreted the same way: a fear of our own attraction to the racial other.

Unlike Neville, Anita manages to overcome this initial fear. By *Burnt Offerings*, she is sleeping with Jean-Claude, albeit with some guilt:

> Good girls do not have premarital sex, especially with the undead. . . . But here I was, doing it. Me, Anita Blake,

> turned into coffin bait. Sad, very sad. . . . You can't trust
> anyone who sleeps with the monsters.

If Anita's relationship with Jean-Claude was just sexual, it could
be characterized as racist, as a sexual objectification of the racial other. But, it clearly becomes much more than that, as evident in the
following passage in *Blue Moon*:

> But I did spare a thought for how that might make my
> vampire lover feel. His heart didn't always beat, but it could
> still break. That's love. Sometimes it feels good. Sometimes
> it's just another way to bleed.

Although their relationship is by no means monogamous, Anita
clearly considers Jean-Claude's feelings and labels her own emotional
response as "love." Theirs is a relationship driven in part by sexual
gratification, but it is not exploitative, not objectifying. Despite the
age difference,[6] Anita's growing powers allow her relationship with
Jean-Claude (and other non-humans) to be characterized by neither
contempt (as when Dracula represents the East European immigrant)
nor jealousy (as when Dracula represents the Jew). Unlike the vampire hunters who preceded her, Anita genuinely connects with the
racial other. Changing times indeed.

Under the Surface

Yet, like in our own world, racial elements do brew underneath the
surface and illustrate several problematic aspects of contemporary
race relations. For one, there is the troublesome fact that Anita still
identifies, in part, as a vampire hunter and consults regularly with the
Regional Preternatural Investigation Taskforce (RPIT), a special division of the police department dedicated to protecting humans from
non-humans. A police division targeting only the minority segment
of the population is reminiscent of COINTELPRO, the FBI's top-se-
cret Counter Intelligence Program that formally operated between

---

[6] In the Anita Blake universe, age equals power.

1956 and 1971. COINTELPRO was originally formed to disrupt the activities of the U.S. Communist Party but is best known for targeting Black nationalist groups ranging from the Black Panthers to the National Association for the Advancement of Colored People (NAACP) through illegal surveillance, infiltration, psychological warfare, legal harassment, and illegal force and violence. In the case of radical Black and Puerto Rican activists, COINTELPRO's actions were so extensive, vicious, and calculated that, according to attorney Brian Glick, they can accurately be termed a form of official "terrorism." It's true, of course, that Dolph, Zerbrowski, and the rest of the RPIT squad all operate within the confines of the law, but it is nevertheless telling that the police department, an arm of the government, needs a special division to cope with the vampire threat.

Another indication of racial tension is the existence of several anti-vampire groups, such as the League of Human Voters and Humans Against Vampires (HAV), both of which purportedly work within the legal system to agitate against vampire rights. These groups are clear parallels to real-world organizations, such as the Council of Conservative Citizens (which promotes racial segregation and condemns interracial marriage) and VDARE (which advocates reduced immigration).[7] A more extreme right-wing racial element is represented in the Anita Blake novels by the KKK-inspired Humans First, a group that originated within Humans Against Vampires but uses violence rather than the legal methods preferred by HAV.

These parallels are intentionally drawn, but they are too obvious to be intended metaphorically. That is, Hamilton uses a variety of historical and contemporary realities to bring her fictional world to life. Indeed, one of the pleasures of reading the Anita Blake novels is the recognition of our own world, including its geographic landscape,

---

[7] It is worth noting that just as vampires are often metaphors for the contemporary threat in novels, so are they in non-fictional discourse. Consider as evidence the frequent online references to immigrants sucking the resources of the host community (e.g., Rojas) or the following "definition" of an ACLU attorney found in an online blog: "A soulless creature that cowers at the sight of a crucifix and lives by sucking money from the government. . . . Refuses to be seen in any media interview, since the glaring light of truth shone upon the world through an honest question is the ACLU Lawyers equivalent of a mirror" (from the blog *Ravings of a Mad Tech*).

its political structures, and yes, its hate groups. Unlike Stoker and Matheson, who seemed to intend their novels to be read on both literal and metaphorical levels, it is unlikely that Hamilton ever had such an intention. That the metaphor retains its meaning despite that is really a testament to the power of the vampire archetype developed in *Dracula* and built up over the past 100 years.

Beyond the Metaphor

We can, to be sure, step outside the metaphor and examine racial dynamics in the Anita Blake novels on a literal level. Anita of course is White. Sort of. Her mother's family emigrated from Mexico, but she was raised by her father's German family after her mother died and, for all practical purposes, she comes across as a typical (in a racial/ethnic sense) White woman.[8] Also noteworthy in this regard is that all of Anita's friends and lovers (human or otherwise) are White, too—this in St. Louis, a city that is over 51 percent African American according to the 2000 Census.[9] There are, to be sure, a handful of non-White characters, including her mentor Manny Rodriguez,[10] but other than Manny, none have prominent roles and only Luther, a human bartender who works the day shift at Dead Dave's,[11] is ever essential to the plot.[12] As such, Luther can be seen as the series' sym-

---

[8] I actually must confess that I missed Anita Blake's Mexican background entirely in my own reading and was alerted to this by this book's fine editor, who also generously shared with me her inspiration for Anita's full assimilation into Whiteness.

[9] It is also worth noting that, like many U.S. cities, St. Louis was historically segregated, with north St. Louis being primarily African American and South St. Louis City primarily White. It is not evident from the books' description whether the Vampire District is located in the north or south.

[10] Others include Yasmeen, a master vampire (*Circus of the Damned*); Vivian, a wereleopard (*Burnt Offerings, Narcissus in Chains*); Rashida, a werewolf (*Circus of the Damned*); and Jamison Clarke, a fellow animator at Animators, Inc. (*Guilty Pleasures, The Laughing Corpse*).

[11] A bar in the district owned by a vampire and ex-cop by the same name. Luther was last seen working there in *The Laughing Corpse*.

[12] It is worth noting that in contemporary U.S. race relations, the Black-White paradigm is so dominant that other racialized groups, including Latinos, Asians, and Native Americans, are often rendered invisible. Despite over ten years of work in racial studies, I too am sometimes guilty of this and am grateful to BenBella's Leah Wilson for remind-

bolic representation of the racial other, in general, and blackness, in particular. Indeed, unlike other non-White characters, Hamilton takes some extra effort to establish his blackness. In *Guilty Pleasures*, Luther is not merely Black; he is "a very dark black man, nearly purplish black, like mahogany." But apart from his Blackness and his friendliness with Anita, we know nothing about Luther's inner world or even what he does away from work.

Luther thus may offer a final window into how the Anita Blake novels represent contemporary race relations. White Americans have mostly rejected the explicit racism and anti-Semitism found in *Dracula* and have mainly turned away from the anti-miscegenation attitudes personified by Robert Neville in *I Am Legend*. It's probably not a stretch to say that the majority of White Americans, like their Black counterparts, honestly want a racially just, egalitarian society. No doubt Hamilton falls squarely in this camp. What the character of Luther reminds us is that true racial justice also requires racial intimacy, a deep knowledge and familiarity with those who are not part of the racial in-group.[13] Without such familiarity, there is no real recognition and, therefore, no real opportunity to interact as equals. Hamilton clearly gets this, for Anita's prejudices against vampires waned as she got to know some of them intimately. But it is telling that, in our current racial fabric, many of us,[14] like Anita, seem to have greater familiarity with vampires than with some of our human neighbors.

---

ing me that Manny's personal and religious connection to the Vaudun priestess in *The Laughing Corpse* was an integral and culturally significant part of the storyline. At the same time (and despite the recent anti-immigration sentiments directed at Americans of Mexican descent), it is Blackness that continues to be the primary representation of the "racial other."

[13] It is important to note that this emphasis on recognition and valuing of cultural differences is a drastic departure from the ideology of most white conservatives who tend to locate racial justice in color-blindness, a way of interacting with non-Whites as though race had no meaning.

[14] I am speaking here as a part of the White racial majority.

◆   ◆   ◆

Dr. Mikhail Lyubansky is a lecturer in the Department of Psychology at the University of Illinois, Urbana-Champaign, where he teaches Psychology of Race and Ethnicity and Theories of Psychotherapy and writes an occasional essay for BenBella. His research interests focus on conditions associated with beliefs about race, ethnicity, and nationality, especially in immigrant and racial minority populations. He writes a weekly blog (*Between the Lines*) on racial issues for *Psychology Today* and recently co-authored a book about Russian-Jewish immigration: *Building a Diaspora: Russian Jews in Israel, Germany, and the USA*. Thanks to this essay, as well as a previous BenBella essay on *Buffy*, his students are now convinced that "he has a thing for vampires." But, of course!

It's only been in the last few years, the last few Anita Blake novels, that I've realized why it was almost inevitable that I would write about someone who dealt with death. My mother died when I was six. She was only twenty-nine. My grandmother, her mother, never recovered from her death and I spent my childhood with my grandmother making sure I didn't forget it either. I loved my mother, but due to my grandmother's obsession with the tragedy I was never allowed to heal or come to terms with it. Her obsession with the one death would lead eventually to an obsession with death in general, but I'll talk about that later.

The first Anita Blake short story, "Those Who Seek Forgiveness," was all about Anita's zombie raising abilities, a bereaved wife, and a vengeful zombie. The story would eventually see print in my short story anthology, *Strange Candy*. The cemetery that I set the story in was the cemetery that my mother is buried in, because when I sat down to write the story and needed a place to set it I knew that graveyard. I knew it well, because my grandmother saw the treatment of the gravesite as a testament to her love for my mother. I remember cleaning out the carvings on the tombstone with a toothbrush when I was a child. We planted flowers, and every holiday had its grave decoration. I didn't think about why that first Anita story was set there, other than convenience. I mean, what other cemetery did I know as well as that one? It was simply logical.

But my interest in the dead wasn't just about dead relatives. I was raised on real-life ghost stories, from experiences that my older relatives had had with a haunted house they lived in when my aunts and uncles were little to a graveyard story that was right out of *The Twilight Zone*. My grandmother told the stories as gospel. Ghosts were real; that was just the truth. No topic of death or mayhem was considered too harsh for me as a child. I never remember my grandmother protecting me from anything in that vein. She did consider it too much to discuss money with me until I was fifteen or sixteen, but not death. Death, abuse, mental illness, and everything else were fair game. Okay, money and sex were not talked about, but violence was cool as a topic. Again, it seems inevitable that I'd write about a character who embraces violence so freely, but not sex. You can leave your childhood behind but it leaves a mark, one that usually scars.

I'm told by my aunts and uncles that my grandmother, their mother, was more cheerful when she was younger, but I missed that part of her life. I got her when she was morbid, and a very dark personality. The glass wasn't just half empty, it was a cracked, dirty glass and wasn't there something floating in the bottom? I inherited that dark outlook, but have worked for years to be the most optimistic pessimist I know.

But let me leave you with my grandmother's obsession with death. I said it grew to encompass more than just my mother's death. Grandmother got the gifts that most grandmothers get, like Whitman Sampler boxes of chocolate. She had two that hadn't contained chocolate in years, but she kept them and filled them with obituaries. Not ones of friends or family, though those might be in there. She collected obits that were particularly pitiful, or tragic in some way. Then when I visited she would get them out and read them to me, or try to get me to read them, because they were sad or horrible. This is the woman who raised me. So is it any wonder that I grew up to write books about a necromancer who gains power through death?

—*Laurell*

Death Becomes Her

The Role of Anita's Necromancy

SHARON ASHWOOD

Y ou'd think being the Executioner would be enough to warn the vampires off, but in the very first scene of *Guilty Pleasures*, Willie McCoy is sitting in Anita's office asking for help. Apparently the undead are slow to take a hint. Anita ends the conversation by falling back on police protocol and her own personal rules. Anita doesn't work for vampires, she kills them. Period.

It's a good thing Anita has a code, because she's about to progress down a nasty-looking path. Over the course of the books, the obstacles Anita encounters force her to up the ante—whether in terms of magic or her tolerance for violence—to cope with whatever emergency is at hand. Those crises are usually bloody. Each time she pushes those boundaries, she looks more like the monsters she's fighting, whether they're human or preternatural. Eventually the niceties of conventional morality start falling away. By *Obsidian Butterfly* she's nearly level with Edward in the stone-cold-killer sweepstakes and has more monsters at her beck and call than a D-movie film director.

So why doesn't all that power—both magical and plain old Edwardesque violence—push Anita wholly to the dark side? What's stopping her from becoming the high priestess of lustful evil that Dolph seems to fear? The answer lies in who—and also what—Anita is.

Fun with Zombies

Anita does not begin life as an average, happy-go-lucky, white-bread kid—or at least she doesn't stay that way for long. Anita's mother—a first death that never quite gets laid to rest—bequeathed both dark beauty and exotic power to a daughter marooned in a blond, WASP, suburban household. This sets Anita apart from "regular people" from the very beginning. That and, um, accidentally raising corpses from time to time—a fact her father ignores and her stepmother, Judith, deplores. "I won't go into details," Anita relates, "but does the term 'road kill' have any significance for you? It did for Judith. I looked like a nightmare version of the Pied Piper" (*The Laughing Corpse*).

If there was any question in young Anita's mind that her preternatural powers were morally suspect, that doubt is quickly confirmed. Early on, her father takes her to see her Grandmother Flores, a Vaudun priestess, to help her control her talents. Grandma's response is that it's "hard to be Vaudun and a necromancer and not be evil" (*The Laughing Corpse*). Then, just to iron in the family neurosis, Anita is cut off from her mother's kin for the good of her soul.

The "zombie queen" stigma was bound to leave a mark. There is no sense of freedom or self-abandonment in Anita. She enters adulthood with a fierce need for internal control that at times borders on repression. A church-goer, she doesn't drink, smoke, or do drugs. She cringes at the idea of Catherine's bachelorette party and doesn't like the idea of being a bridesmaid any better. She doesn't dance in public and, even twelve books later in *Incubus Dreams*, only agrees to do so at Larry's wedding under duress. She's obviously more comfortable with guns than her feminine side and hates showing anything resembling vulnerability or weakness. Notably, after a disastrous college affair, she has no appetite to risk that kind of rejection again. Until well into the series, Anita sleeps alone.

These uncompromising aspects of her character are significant, because her self-control is often what is challenged. Even more important: it's her softer side she's trying to protect by repressing, the one that does nurture and love; that's often her saving grace.

She makes one large compromise, and that's her profession. Anita learned early on that she has to use her animating ability or it will use itself, raising the dead at random. So, unable to reject her talents entirely, Anita becomes an animator but takes a carefully ethical path. She's a pain in her boss's rear end, but a straight-shooter with the clients and their deceased. Despite her abilities, she dislikes animators who abuse or exploit the dead and enlists Irving's help to push for zombie-rights legislation. At the start of *Guilty Pleasures*, the Anita we meet has already laid the foundation for her future role in the preternatural community. The dead are a key part of her life and she treats them well—as long as they're behaving themselves.

Equally significant is her job as Executioner. Anita has been taught from childhood to see her abilities as dangerous, so her affinity for the dead is paired with a need to police its power. Anita's animating ability extends to vampires. This means she can guess their age and power, and she's harder to hypnotize. In the opening scene with Willie McCoy, she sees them as creatures to be avoided or, if they get uppity enough, blown to smithereens. It's not a huge leap to see how this parallels her attitude toward her own abilities. Anita keeps herself on a short leash. She demands the same restraint from the vamps as she does from herself.

From Animator to Necromancer

The dead waste no time in challenging Anita's rules. She refuses to work for Nikolaos's vampires, so they take her friend, Catherine, hostage through hypnosis. Typically, as adamant as Anita is about what she will and won't do, a friend's safety takes precedence and she takes the case. As a result, the Executioner becomes the vampires' reluctant partner. This first adventure features a triumvirate of circumstances—a friend in need, Anita breaking her rules, and Anita gaining power (in this case, vampire marks)—that we see time and again throughout the books.

Narcissus in Chains contains another such example: Anita rescues the wereanimals from Chimera, has—very uncharacteristically—sex with a stranger, Micah, when the *ardeur* rises, and forges a much deeper personal and mystical bond with the leopards. In *The Killing Dance*, despite her reservations about playing human servant, Anita agrees to form the triumvirate to ensure the safety of Richard and Jean-Claude, and discovers that she has the ability to raise sleeping vampires. It is often through risking herself in defense of another that Anita gains strength. In particular, when Anita allies herself with the dead, she increases her power.

The same pattern repeats when Anita runs up against the Vaudun priestess, Dominga Salvador, in *The Laughing Corpse*. This time we see Anita really come into her own, magically speaking, but on her own terms. At first Dominga tries to tempt Anita by offering to teach her all those things Grandmother Flores struck from the curriculum, but Anita's not interested. She won't seek power that she considers corrupt—not even when that magic could be considered her birthright. When Anita does finally break out of the role of vanilla animator, it's because lives are at stake. As the battle with Dominga goes critical, Anita taps into her neglected necromancy at long last, embracing her connection to the dead. It's a key moment; this deeper connection with her abilities is a leap forward in Anita's phenomenal power growth. It also revives a long-standing question: Will a taste of Anita's inherited talents send her hurtling to the dark side?

Not this time. Although Anita discovers just how great high-voltage magic feels, she does not go power-mad. What she's seen of Dominga, who torments zombies, disgusts Anita. Her basic empathy for the dead keeps her from following that corrupt path. Instead she uses what she's learned to be a better animator. If the forces of darkness want Anita's soul, they're going to have to up their game.

Blue *Munin* and Other Health Issues: Anita as Healer

After the Dominga incident, Anita's on a roll. Each subsequent book sees her with an increasingly well-stocked magical arsenal, and by the time we reach *Blue Moon* and *The Killing Dance*, Anita is firmly entangled with the preternatural community and gaining new powers through those associations. What's clear, though, is that regardless of what talents she acquires, her own necromancy remains her central power. In fact, it's often her sympathy with death that draws new power to her.

Anita's adventures with the Tennessee wolves is a case in point. The pack has tied their *munin*, the collective memory of their dead, to their lupenar with blood and death magic. The description of their lupenar in *Blue Moon* is striking: It has an old oak tree covered with the bones of their pack members. From the moment Anita arrives, she feels an affinity with the place, and she gathers strength from the *munin* when she makes her move against Colin's rotting vampires. Those she doesn't fry; she explodes them with Edward-worthy spectacle. With this incident, Anita shows that, despite her growing entanglement with other power sources, her necromancy is a significant force all on its own. If Anita wants to be a supernatural bad-ass, she can do that all by herself.

However, Anita does adopt other types of magic. A good example is Raina's *munin*, which Anita is able to access through her connection to Richard and his wolves. It comes at a price: Anita is afraid it will tempt her to kill more easily. Because of Raina's highly sexualized personality, it also is linked to lust, not an easy burden for the restrained Anita. But the *munin* has its uses. Anita raises it for the first time in *Burnt Offerings*, when she heals Nathaniel. Although the power summons a dark urge to crush his heart "until blood flowed and his life stopped," Anita resists both violent and sexual temptation and channels the energy to heal his injuries.

This passage is another defining moment for Anita. She uses a potentially destructive power—one that urges her to use it for her own dark gratification—to give aid to someone else. Once she can focus it, Raina's *munin* becomes, at least for a few books, one of Anita's most valuable tools.

Since death magic is Anita's home base, it's no surprise that she is able to use her necromancy in a similar fashion. As soon as her triumvirate with Jean-Claude and Richard is formed, Anita learns that she can use her abilities to not only raise and control vampires when they're asleep, but also to heal them. In *The Killing Dance*, she fixes Damian's cut with her power, much in the same way she restores zombies to a living appearance. It's telling that, to heal the living she has to harness an outside force, but to heal the dead, the ability comes from within.

The sudden development of this vampire-raising/repairing power gives Jean-Claude pause. After all, he's discovered his human quasi-servant has the ability to make any of his people (and probably him) do whatever she commands while they're snoozing. If Anita had a taste for practical jokes, he would be in a whole new undead hell. Anita enjoys the moment of Jean-Claude's realization. She's not immune to the satisfaction of finally having a hold over the Master of the City. However, Anita focuses her newfound ability on finding a means to heal Sabin. Once again, despite a major leap in mojo, Anita turns away from abusing her power over the dead—alas for fans of low comedy.

There is another way in which Anita heals, and it is far simpler and more primal than any of her other magics. A necromancer's blood, like that of a lycanthrope, holds more power than a human's for the vampire who consumes it. How willing Anita is to share that power changes over time. It's a no-brainer that the Anita we meet at the beginning of *Guilty Pleasures* is unlikely to donate blood voluntarily. However, in *Bloody Bones*, Anita (after some internal debate) and Jason revive Jean-Claude by feeding him. In fact, they overdo it a bit and he becomes slightly drunk. In *Blue Moon*, at different times Anita saves both Damian and Asher. The image of Anita nourishing the vampires with her necromancy-laced blood is a striking portrayal of her complex intimacy with the dead. She does it out of love and friendship, but, as Asher observes, it also gives her power over those she saves. It's only her intentions that keep the act benign.

Nec-Romance: Love Sucks, and It Bites, Too

Intimacy issues are front and center with Anita throughout the series. In some ways, Edward, significantly nicknamed Death, is easier for her to cope with because there is no question of sex between them. Anita's quite content to have a quasi-sociopathic contract killer as a BFF. Edward might be scary, but their relationship is emotionally straightforward. It only starts to look complicated once he reveals his personal life. The fact that he has successfully found one underscores Anita's own uneasiness when it comes to matters of the heart.

Personal relationships, particularly love, force the revelation of one's vulnerabilities. For Anita, loss of control over herself and her powers—either through temptation or through more forcible psychic interference—is fraught with problems. Vampires are extra scary because they are master manipulators, and there is always the hazard that Anita might end up as the pet necromancer of an unscrupulous master.

Lucky for Jean-Claude that Anita likes him. Who else could have escaped unscathed while marking her as his servant, threatening her boyfriend, and otherwise making a total pest of himself? No one can make Anita cross her own lines in the sand like Jean-Claude. At the beginning of the series, she's quick to remind him that he's just a pretty walking corpse, but her defenses don't hold forever. Not only does he appeal to her as a woman, but her power responds to his nature.

Necromancy loves the dead, and the dead love it right back. This is made utterly plain by the rhapsodic way Anita describes her feelings for Jean-Claude:

> I felt his stillness, a depth of quiet that nothing living could touch, like a still pool of water hidden away in the dark. In one crystalline moment, I realized that, for me, this was part of the attraction: I wanted to plunge my hands into his stillness, into that quiet place of death. I wanted to embrace it, confront it, conquer it. I wanted to fill him up with a burning wash of life, and I knew in that moment that I could do it, but only at the price of drinking in some of that still, dark water. (*The Killing Dance*)

The language sums up the push and pull between them. Jean-Claude comes to love Anita, but her powers are never far from his mind. More than once the question is raised as to who, in the end, will be the master and who will be the servant. His initial courtship of Anita is as much a pre-emptive strike as anything else.

As their complicated relationship takes shape, so does Anita's bond with vampire magic. The longer she stays with Jean-Claude, the richer and more interconnected their preternatural skills become. The most influential gift he passes to Anita is the *ardeur*, which allows her to feed on lust. She becomes a succubus and, much to her embarrassment, she's soon raising up more than zombies.

Life as a succubus has logistical challenges, including making enough whoopee to keep the members of her triumvirate, Nathaniel and particularly Damian, from fading away. The blending of necromancy and vampirism here is plain. It's supposed to be her zombie-raising talents that animate Damian, but it's feeding the *ardeur* that gives her the energy to keep him going. This is taken further when Anita improves Damian's looks during the triumvirating process, which, in an oddly Darwinian fashion, gives him an increased ability to attract female attention and thus food. Jean-Claude links Anita's necromantic and vampiric abilities when he identifies this "makeover" power as one of Belle Morte's, although Belle could only use it on new vampires. He says, "[T]his is a new ability altogether . . . What if you have gained abilities through your necromancy that we cannot begin to guess at?" (*Incubus Dreams*).

Good question. Why has any of this power-hybridization happened, and why does it manifest the way it does? The connection between necromancy and vampires seems relatively logical given the death/dead connection, but the fact that the *ardeur* informs Anita's blended magic is almost poignant. After all, Anita loves Jean-Claude, and her affinity is with the dead. Isn't it logical that her hybrid powers, fuelled as they are with all of her will and passion, would find a way to nourish and enhance those closest to her? She's turned every other power gain into a means of helping others. Why not this one?

In fact, the *ardeur* does mutate, allowing her to see the strongest need in someone's heart. Consciously or unconsciously, Anita responds to those needs, as in her relationships with Micah and Nathaniel. Furthermore, whoever sleeps with Anita gains in magic—a fact not lost on Rafael, who begins to think the rats will lose out if he doesn't stake a claim as one of Anita's bedmates. She turns what is essentially a method of feeding into a means to protect and nurture.

Not that it's all group hugs. Anita is still playing with monsters, and Grandmother Flores's dire predictions about Anita's magic hold a glimmer of truth. Despite the strength it gives Anita, combining powers with the vampires isn't comfortable. Besides the whole succubus gig—an ongoing complication in Anita's domestic life—the vampire/necromancer power blend gives Anita some very dark abilities. She sucks the life out of Chimera, she rolls Avery as well as any master vamp could, and she blood-oaths Malcolm's entire flock. She seizes control of Augustine of Chicago—significant even if he was a willing victim. With Jean-Claude, she feeds off all of Augustine's entourage.

While this über-necrovampmancy allows Anita to save the day time and again, its sheer force frightens her deeply. In the end, she's so afraid of losing herself in power and harming others that she makes Wicked and Truth promise to kill her if she goes bad. All along she's been the Executioner; now she's seeking out someone else to enforce her sense of order if she can't. The moment is telling, especially when one thinks back to that first scene with Willie McCoy, and how Anita was afraid to even look him in the eyes. She's come a long way, but it wasn't a comfy ride.

Hell's Belles

The degree to which Anita is spooked by her own power may seem extreme, but book after book she battles with two prima donnas of vampire evil, Belle Morte and Marmee Noir, who are prime examples of two of Anita's greatest fears: how she could degenerate if she falls—as Grandmother Flores so desperately feared she would—to the temptation of her own dark talents, and the more immediate danger, that she could be lost to the control of someone willing to use those powers for their own nefarious schemes.

Belle Morte, or Beautiful Death, is, by virtue of her name alone, an appropriate adversary for a necromancer. Animators seem to have a particular affinity for Belle Morte, since both Anita and Larry, for an unexplained reason, can at times catch her signature rose scent when no one else can. She is a mirror for Anita—after all, Anita has Belle's *ardeur*, her ability to call leopards, and is sleeping with quite a few of Belle's men. The parallel is not lost on the vampire, who at various points in time tries to take the leopards and the men back.

But given Belle's seniority in the vampire realm, is this perceived similarity/rivalry superficial? Is Anita a potential mini-Morte? The answer is yes in terms of power and no in terms of personality. Anita already gives Belle a run for her money, using necromancy to cast her out time and again. Whenever Belle attacks the people Anita cares for, such as Asher, Anita's will to fight back just gets stronger. As Anita's hybridized powers grow, it's possible that one day she could defeat Belle outright. Where any true similarity stops is that Anita's motivations are nowhere near the same as Belle's. Anita may be pragmatic and ruthless, she may no longer buy into truth, justice, and the American way, but she's not going to become a narcissistic nightmare. The very fact that Anita is prepared to die first at the hands of Wicked and Truth is proof enough.

Marmee Noir, the original vampire, is a different kind of threat. Unlike Belle, she doesn't bother with seduction and power games. The Mother of All Darkness represents the ultimate loss of self. It's not enough that Anita has to worry about sliding over onto the dark side; Marmee Noir wants to save time and simply take her over.

By *Skin Trade* it's clear that possession is on the menu. Marmee's physical body has atrophied during her long rest, and Anita is a prime candidate for a replacement vessel. After all, they share vampirism, cat lycanthropy, and necromancy, as well as other talents, such as the ability to break the bond between master and servant. No wonder Anita interests Mommie Dearest enough to rouse her from sleep. Marmee Noir's own laws dictated that all necromancers be put to death, so it's unlikely that as suitable a match will ever come along again, whether for full possession or as a tide-me-over snack-bar until she finds a less-intransigent host. It's almost as if Marmee Noir is Anita with her darkest powers fully realized, ready to step into a fresh incarnation.

Marmee Noir's effect on Anita is significant, in part because their similarities give Marmee a way inside. She touches Anita through her beasts, both by giving her the tigers and by landscaping Anita's inner zoo, whether intentionally or accidentally, in the image of a primordial forest. If Mommie Dearest is redecorating the inside of Anita's head, she's definitely planning on moving in.

At the end of *Skin Trade*, it looks like Marmee Noir won't get to carry out her scheme, but only future books will tell whether the

Mother of All Darkness is truly out of the picture. We're left with some interesting questions: Is the ultimate darkness that easy to kill? If her spirit was already separated from her body, where did the spirit go?

More to the point: At the rate Anita's powers are growing, what will she become? Is Anita's concern for others enough to keep her from heading down the highway to Evil Divadom? The answer is almost certainly yes, but the possibility of disaster is always provocative. After all, who could have predicted Anita's journey thus far?

In Death We Trust

Anita's necromancy is central to who and what she is from the start; for her, there never was a fully human existence. "All the monsters start out normal except me," she ruefully observes (*The Laughing Corpse*). As a child, Anita's family assumes her abilities are a precursor to evil, and that assumption has a predictable effect. Anita walls herself behind rules around her magic and her personal behavior. Those boundaries are, however. constantly renegotiated: Anita's most significant gains are made when she invites the dead to become her ally. Through this alliance we see that Anita's moral compass is not just a stumbling block en route to world domination. Anita treats the dead with respect. She loves and protects them. She sleeps with them. She'll even feed them her blood to keep them vibrantly undead.

That affinity and affection keeps Anita from succumbing to the dark side. Just as well, because there's no escape for her, according to the Mother of All Darkness: "The dead give necromancers no peace. We pester the poor things, because they draw us like moths to the flame" (*The Harlequin*).

◆   ◆   ◆

Sharon Ashwood is a freelance journalist, novelist, desk jockey, and enthusiast for the weird and spooky. She has an English literature degree but works as a finance geek. Interests include growing her to-be-read pile and playing with the toy graveyard on her desk. As a vegetarian, she freely admits the whole vampire/werewolf lifestyle fantasy would never work out, so she writes paranormal romances instead. Sharon lives in the Pacific Northwest and is owned by the Demon Lord of Kitty Badness.

Anita Blake worries about whether she's a sociopath, a bad guy, from the beginning of the series. As she struggles to be honorable in a world that keeps forcing her to be ever more ruthless and deadly just to survive and protect those weaker than herself, she worries that the price she pays is her soul. In the early books she's worried that if she becomes a vampire she'll literally lose her immortal soul, but as the series goes on she meets too many vampires who are less scary and less horrible than the human beings. She finds that a pair of fangs doesn't keep you from having a heart of gold, and having a heartbeat doesn't mean you aren't a heartless bastard.

When the monsters are better friends to you than the people is that a sign that the monsters aren't bad guys or that you've become one of the monsters? Anita thinks about that a lot. In the recent book *Skin Trade*, she goes to Vegas to hunt a serial killer vampire, Vittorio. But her backup is Edward, nicknamed Death by the vampires, and Olaf, serial killer in his own right. They've both been backup for Anita before, and when two of the scariest human beings we've ever met are on our side, are we still the good guy? How can you be on the side of the angels when the devils are your right and left hand? If your closest friends are monsters and sociopaths what does that say about you as a person? When you only feel safe in relationships with people who turn furry once a month, or live on a diet of blood, what does that say about you?

Anita is embracing herself and that self seems to be very comfortable with the others of society, the outcasts, the ones who all the good people tell us are monsters. She finds more acceptance and safety with them than with normal humans. Why? I know that part of it is that the monsters are tougher and less easy to kill, and with my early tragic losses I really value that. And since Anita shares some of my background she values it, too. But in the first book, *Guilty Pleasures*, she loses Phillip. She loses someone that she said she'd protect. The monsters kill him and she can't save him and that haunts her. I promised her that I would never kill another man whom she loved, or almost loved. Sometimes I think she started to collect the men so I couldn't kill them off.

Or maybe I did it; maybe I wanted in my fiction a little more life and a little less death. It sounds funny in a series that is all about death, but being a vampire isn't true death. It's not sit-in-the-coffin-and-rot death, it's rise up at night and be beautiful and eternal and not worry about that whole afterlife thing because you're already living it. I believe sincerely in an afterlife, and reincarnation, but there is that part of me that was so scarred by that first death when I was only six that it still longs for an alternative, an alternative where the person you love still walks, still talks, and is still the same person you loved forever. Is it a child's wish? Yes. But I think it's a child's wish that none of us really outgrow. I know I never did.

—Laurell

Death's Got Your Back

When Edward and the
Big Bad Heavies Are on Your Team

VERA NAZARIAN

OLAF: I'll take the head.
ANITA: I'll take the heart.
—*Obsidian Butterfly*

When you're Anita Blake, U.S. Marshal and legally sanctioned Vampire Hunter, you have one hell of a complicated relationship with everyone else in your world. There's rarely any time to get to know the other, so you shoot first and ask questions later.

You have regular run-of-the-mill enemies, really serious enemies, and super-badass enemies. And when the monsters themselves call you "The Executioner"—stressing "The" and adding capitalized emphasis—it's not even a matter of an inability to have friends, it's simply that for everyone's sake you can't afford to have any. Besides, all the men you get intimate with are not always easily definable as friends or lovers, and you prefer things to remain vague that way.

But work still needs to get done. And in your lonely, friendless line of work . . . well, that's when you have to take unsavory sides, make alliances. You agree to temporary personal ceasefires with people (okay, not always *people*) you wouldn't normally trust to be in the same room with you without a loaded gun. . . . And such dangerous compromise not only sucks O-Neg but blows undead chunks.

But it makes for great story.

When Laurell K. Hamilton started writing the now wildly popular Anita Blake books, beginning with *Guilty Pleasures*, she brought to life an amazing and fascinating character and arguably created a previously unseen archetype, that of a hardboiled law-woman with a ruthless attitude and supernatural abilities. These days, pale Anita knockoffs are a dime a dozen, and indeed a whole new "urban paranormal" genre has sprung up and flourished like spilled zombie guts.

But there's only one Anita Blake. The one, the original. And what makes her unique is her complex and conflicted personality—a combination of a deeply hidden, vulnerable and sensitive "juicy liquid" interior (which is the true source of her personal and necromancer powers), and the hard-as-diamond, cold, rock-candy-shell exterior. Granted, a crusty shell is not as uncommon in male noir detectives, or even in tough dames, but few can claim to be so ruthless on the outside as Anita. This outer mask is almost masculine, in the traditional hardboiled genre sense, and made up of standoffish, aggressive, attack-dog anger. Throw in a good measure of brutal honesty and a faithful heart, and make her a control freak and an occasional bitch with the best intentions. What an explosive powerhouse!

We've already mentioned that, except for Edward, Anita has no real friends. (Ronnie Sims doesn't count; she was the "girly" normal friend and workout partner in the earlier books, making fewer and fewer appearances as time went on. But we all know how little Anita really shared with her, even in that initial need to keep up appearances of personal and social normalcy, which she basically gave up as her story progressed, together with friends, youthful illusions, and those stuffed penguins—whatever happened to the penguin collection? Does Nathaniel get to dust off the penguins when it's his turn for house chores?) However, she does have a large number of sweeties (Micah, Nathaniel, and Jean-Claude probably being the most "normal" friend/lover-level intimates), and a whole extended solar system of various sex-partner "satellites" and succubus-food (*pomme de sang* volunteers; to be blunt, fuck buddies) that her *ardeur* has condemned her to collect, often against her will, until she learned to get a grip on it (more or less). None of the guys can be regarded as friends in the traditional reciprocal relationship sense. Mostly they're supernatural or otherwise non-human creatures who can take care of themselves (so no easy vulnerability that an enemy can use against Anita) and are neither official life partners nor colleagues—Anita does not like to label her relationships, and that way keeps things safely undefined.

But Anita's romantic relationships are not under discussion here because, let's face it, they're pretty simple—simply impossible, that is. Keeping all your significant others in a chronic state of confused uncertainty, and frequently rejecting them after intimacy? Making them get in line, or adding them to rotation lists, for nookie? Impossible relationships indeed, on every level. Anita tends to make them so, desperately afraid to lose control and let go all the way, then letting go all the way (at which point huge, power-surge magic usually happens and bad guys take a hit together with the sweeties), then again holding back, then . . . well it's an emotional yo-yo.

And with such a predictable back-and-forth on Anita's self-control, it becomes kind of more interesting to see Anita handle the other kind of relationships—the antagonistic ones, where control need never be voluntarily relinquished.

Indeed, some of the most interesting and *unpredictable* tension in the Anita Blake series occurs in the interactions Anita has with her most dangerous allies, and in the moments of crossing the line to work together with her enemies.

So we come to Edward, the scary, almost inhuman friend, who understands Anita unlike anyone else without being romantically involved with her. He's Death who's got her back.

And now let's take it further and bring in the serial killer, Olaf. And why stop there? Let's pull in Belle Morte. And finally, the big bad Mother of All Darkness, Marmee Noir.

Because Anita Blake has, at one point or another, teamed up and worked alongside each one of them against a common *other* enemy, as much as she has struggled *against* them previously.

Unbelievable? Not if we take a closer look at Anita's fears and motivations.

Anita has three issues: trust, commitment, and control. Call them a trinity of symptoms of the same affliction, or three different kinds of fruity swirl in the same flavor of ice cream—either way, it can all result in serious brain freeze. Because Anita is incapable of opening herself all the way to anyone, incapable of letting go all the way, and afraid to show her true vulnerability, she has to be always on an edge of some kind. Granted, she is always pushing the edge, going further every time, but it's still not *all the way with no reservations*, and she can live with that—her comfort level.

In the best *The X-Files* sense, Anita trusts no one; she knows better, because she's got the instincts of *both* Mulder and Scully. As for commitment, Anita has more sweeties than a harem, and thus allows herself the luxury of juggling people—needing and caring for each one of them in their own special one-on-one way (and, okay, sometimes several at a time; blame the *ardeur*), but never on an exclusive basis. Remember how we thought the choice would come down to Richard versus Jean-Claude? Ha! We laugh now, thinking back, given all the boys currently in the mix.

And control? Why, that's at the heart of it all. Because control is what lets Anita function in her human-monster world, and that's why she holds on to it so fiercely. Control is the gatekeeper of the psyche, mostly keeping everyone out, and just occasionally giving someone a temporary backstage pass. Once they get "in," it's only to experience the blasted emotional yo-yo that is Anita Blake.

Holding people at arm's length is tricky at best, and even painfully insulting to the other, if you are dealing with sweeties and housemates who expect a modicum of emotional intimacy. But it works great when relationships are undefined, vague, and unspecific. As in: enemy, non-friend, non-lover. You can always reel them in and then bounce them away again, like that yo-yo, with no need for an explanation, without emotional complications. (Not to mention, so many of these guys tend to disappear or "lie low," without repercussions, and with remarkably unhurt feelings, for books at a time. Makes you wonder if they get to wait in that pile with the stuffed penguins for Anita's attention.)

Enemies are excellent for holding at arm's length. Never get too close, but lunge and feint emotionally, psychologically. Do the Safety Dance.

And yet, despite everything—despite *herself*, it might seem—
Anita seems secretly to be looking for consistency, for someone to
trust. She cannot allow herself to open up completely to any of her
formal sweeties, because that would be too scary emotionally. Which
means that enemies are fair game.

And of all the people in her life, Edward comes closest to being
that strange rock of reliability in times of combat and danger.

He's cold, perfectly controlled, ruthless. Steely gaze, empty ex-
pressionless eyes. Sociopathic lack of apparent emotion. Whiplash
reactions and hardcore weapons expertise. Chameleon-like ability
to switch character, as needed, including morphing into his more
friendly alias, that of U.S. Marshal Ted Forrester, regular friendly
good ol' boy.

He's also former dark ops, silent killer, bounty hunter, assassin,
hit man. His only weakness? A fiancée and family who know only a
fraction of the depth of his darkness.

And Edward's possibly the only real friend Anita Blake has.

Did I mention his nickname is Death?

In many ways Edward is really a strange beast, an enemy-friend
hybrid. The definition of enemy is "someone who works against you,"
and yet, isn't there some kind of health warning about fraternizing
with sociopaths? The evolution of Edward's character is unlike any
of the other dangerous big bad heavies in the series. From the start
he is a dangerous mentor and ally, always working on Anita's side of
the fence, but potentially liable to go off like a big bad firecracker if
Anita lights his fuse the wrong way. So far that hasn't happened. And
as the storyline has developed over many volumes, it seems that it is
less likely to. Even if Anita tests him to the limit, my bet is on Edward
staying loyal on a personal level.

Ah, Edward, how I loved you! All throughout the series, from the
very first book when you came onstage as a mysterious, dispassionate
stranger, powerful, dangerous, deadly, and able to turn on Anita at
the drop of a hat or the tiniest change in the wind. . . . Oh, yes, how I
loved you. Because unlike the others, amazingly, startlingly, you were
not a vampire, not a werewolf, not an undead supernatural being of
some sort, but an ordinary *human*. And what a human!

When the story began, Anita was afraid of Edward, and the reader picked it up, a thrilling, creepy, unknown fear thing mixed up with respect, the kind that raises hairs on your scalp and sends shivers down your back—in a terrifying yet sexy way. Back then, Edward was mostly an unknown factor, and as such, he was the third potential romantic object. While Jean-Claude sashayed in vintage silk, dropping "*ma petite*"s, and Richard raved with wolf spittle flying, a number of us Edward fans hoped that a spark might grow between him—Mr. Deadly Cool—and Anita.

And now, looking back, I am so glad it has not. Edward is perfect as he's written; he is the one person who is Anita's anchor of sanity, her onetime skilled combat teacher and master, and now equal. He fills the gap between intimate lover and foe. He is the human wall between the *inside* and the *outside* of Anita's hard shell.

Edward is the personification of Anita's *control*.

And yet, he's Death. And death's this necromancer girl's best friend.

She knows they are potential enemies even when she knows he's her friend. Granted, their relationship is always evolving, and anything can still happen. Edward once admitted to Anita that he'd turned down a hit job where she herself was the target, and instead came down to warn her and offer his protection. He's her brother, her weapon, her sparring partner, and even her confessor. Just as Joss Whedon's Buffy could open up and talk to Spike and tell him her darkness in season 6 of *Buffy the Vampire Slayer*, Anita can tell Edward—the face of her personal demon—the whole terrible truth, always, and expect not intimacy, not love, but perfect understanding. Edward's the cool and reliable mirror of herself. Of all the men in her life, he is probably the most dominant—just as she is. Anita knows this, and it's why she can trust him enough to turn her back on him. Death has always served Anita well; it is the one thing she knows, and the necromancer in her depths knows it profoundly on the metaphysical level.

The extreme opposite of the *reliable danger* in the person of Edward is the *unpredictable danger* of the serial killer and convicted rapist Olaf, a.k.a. Otto Jefferies. Of German decent (Hapsburg), bald, super tall, with silent sleek motions and imposing muscles, Olaf first came on the scene as Edward's hired backup in *Obsidian Butterfly*, then showed up again briefly in *The Harlequin* and more extensively in the most recent *Skin Trade*, in both cases working with Edward and Anita to solve extremely dangerous cases. Between the former and the latter books, Olaf underwent a near-impossible (and immensely entertaining) transformation in his attitude toward Anita Blake.

At first, misogynist Olaf ignored Anita completely as a mere woman, and in the scene of their first meeting, he refused to even respond to her greeting or look at her. Anita of course had to taunt him in her own special way, and they ended up with weapons drawn until Edward came, like Big Bad Dad, to separate them (*Obsidian Butterfly*). The rest of the book is a dissonant dance of uneasy truce and tension, with Anita and Olaf basically always on opposite sides of pieces of furniture, keeping pace and taking out targets—on the same team and yet never getting too close to one another. To make matters worse, Anita discovered that physically she fits Olaf's exact favorite victim profile; truly a girl of his serial killer dreams.

But with each new grim, merciless, ruthlessly necessary act of killing on Anita's part, witnessed by Olaf—who'd only ever disdained women as weak nothings—his attitude changed. He started to see Anita as something more, and grudgingly admitted to her: "You would have made a good man." Which, coming from him, was the highest compliment possible. And Anita, in her own dark way, understood and acknowledged that (*Obsidian Butterfly*). The scene culminates with possibly the most bizarre serial killer romantic moment ever (stand aside, Johnny Depp and Helena Bonham Carter in Tim Burton's movie remake of *Sweeney Todd*), when Anita and Olaf butcher the same monster together, he beheading it and she cutting out the heart, elbow-deep in blood. When she pulls out the heart, Olaf has to touch it. Their fingers and hands connect, and Olaf is smitten. There's almost a kiss (admittedly on Olaf's part only; for Anita, it's an eeow moment).

I don't know if the author giggled when she wrote that scene, since it was so over-the-top, but this reader certainly did, because it was immensely satisfying, in the sickest, wickedest way possible, to have Anita "out-bad" the bad guy and impress a serial killer. Seriously twisted. The Olaf–Anita moment will remain a classic.

I'm not sure exactly when the serial killer protagonist became such a hot trend, culminating in the Showtime TV series *Dexter*. But Olaf has certainly become a fascinating and welcome recurring character for some of us twisted and pervy (pardon my Cassie Clare) readers. In the end of *Obsidian Butterfly*, Olaf wrote Anita a note—ahem, love letter—before he left, hoping for the opportunity to "hunt" with her again. And it was gleeful wicked fun to see him reprise his role in later volumes, trying to take it to the next level. Laurell K. Hamilton *had* to be giggling when she wrote his interactions with Anita in *Skin Trade*.

But how does Anita feel about dealing with Olaf? With a serial killer partner, she knows exactly what he's capable of, in terms of killing, fighting, weapons, and black ops expertise; and yes, he'll get his part of the job done. She can rely on that, 100 percent. But unlike Edward (dependable, friendly Death, "maybe someday"), she cannot trust Olaf at all on a personal level, and for good reason. She can barely stand next to him without feeling creepy crawlies. Like an unpredictable wild thing, she knows he can and will strike, given the chance. And the other weird thing is, Olaf is a guaranteed twofer: you get death with your love. Or love with your death.

And yet, Olaf represents an extraordinary and fascinating personal challenge for Anita—and yes, on some level, an attraction—of "always holding death at bay." Because with Olaf, death is not just a possibility, but a *sure thing*. Anita knows he's biding his time. She seriously would do her best not to have to get any closer to him on the job, not even when he so gallantly volunteers to feed her *ardeur*—real honest-to-goodness sex that doesn't involve killing his partner! (*Skin Trade*). But him keeping her on her toes is okay; it kind of hones her own deadly skills. And just maybe it reminds her not to go too far into the killer *mindspace*, before she irrevocably loses what's left of her own humanity.

So far we've talked about the big bad human members of Anita's work team. Now let's push the line even further, to the even weirder supernatural baddies, the immortal ones.

Starting with "Beautiful Death," the mother of Jean-Claude's (and hence Anita's) vampire line and sexy succubus powers.

Belle Morte is an enemy, plain and simple. A chronic, clear-cut enemy across the pond, over in the Old Country. She stands for cruelty and sex torture of pretty men and women of all ages, and perfumed satin sheets, and frilly stuff, and, okay, everything Anita fights against and abhors. And yet, she's the mom of all *ardeur*. And *ardeur*, whether Anita likes it or not, is one hell of a powerful weapon. Even if she never asked for it, and kind of got it like metaphysical VD.

Belle Morte, who is first introduced in *Narcissus in Chains*, is only an intangible presence in the books so far, sort of like Charlie's disembodied voice in *Charlie's Angels*. Except, of course, she's a "bizarro-world" evil Charlie in a dominatrix outfit. And she has a very nasty agenda for Anita and the gang.

A powerful member of the Vampire Council, an irresistibly beautiful female vampire with honey-colored eyes and the ability to enhance the beauty of others, she is the one who created Jean-Claude's vampire bloodline, and thus indirectly "infected" Anita. Belle Morte makes contact with Anita in her dreams, or through others like Jean-Claude, during moments of uncontrolled *ardeur*. If sex and death could mix in dark beauty, the offspring would be Belle Morte, the dark goddess of both kinds of id-driven need—undead vampire hunger and living animal lust. She is death with a strange *doubled* life urge, burdened not only with a vampire's basic need for sustenance, but also the sensual desire to love, and, by extension, to propagate and breed (one might say, kind of like a virus). Is it any wonder Belle Morte meddles so in the lives of her children, whom she so *loves*?

Indeed, as the story unfolds, Belle Morte appears to have taken a protective interest in Anita, and her hostile "attacks" have occurred just in the nick of time to distract Anita from some other enemy's bid for psychic possession.

There is never any trust between Anita and Belle Morte, but Anita does realize that the power she offers comes in handy. Anita is ever vigilant and wary of Belle Morte, because she recognizes that—at least in the present balance of power—this terrible, beautiful, ancient vampire is more powerful than Anita is. Full-force, Belle Morte could overwhelm her and make her drown. . . . And yet, she is "family," the terrible-beautiful bloodline, and she is in some ways dark love, the kind of twisted love that Anita can understand on some dysfunctional level (Anita's uncommitted, inconsistent uncertainty toward her guys is only a step away from being genuinely hurtful). And love, used as a weapon (as is done to great effect in the end of *Skin Trade*), is unbeatable.

When Belle Morte infiltrates and infuses Anita with her *ardeur* powers, she basically allies with her against her will, in a strange on-and-off-again, informal, temporary psychic "arrangement." Anita uses Belle Morte's "gift" of extended power to fight off other enemies in the unconventional way of "loving" them to death, of taking away their will and making them hers. It's in some ways the power of the ultimate surprise—the last thing an opponent expects is a kiss instead of a stab—and a dance on the fine edge of control.

Ah, we're back to control, Anita's favorite problem. She has no control over Belle Morte, and is only now coming to basic grips with the *ardeur*. Unlike in her dealings with Edward or Olaf, her human, mortal Scary Team members, she cannot even keep Belle Morte at bay temporarily, when push comes to shove. However, she can *use* Beautiful Death as one does a rare and powerful ability, simply by *allowing her in*.

Allowing in the enemy. Talk about taking it to the edge and crossing the line!

The only problem, then, is how to kick Belle Morte back *out* once the job is done.

And for that Anita has to reach deep inside herself, deeper than the *ardeur* flows, deeper than anything, and "pull out" her inner necromancer. Once again, it's a form of death to the rescue! Death trumps sex.

Indeed, having Belle Morte as an ally is like having raging acres of wildfire as your weapon, and then needing the cold deep water of death itself to put it out. Every. Damn. Time. At the risk of your own existence.

Which brings us to the most interesting, darkest, most elemental enemy-colleague on Anita's Big Bad Dream Team.

Marmee Noir.

The Mother of All Darkness. The Sweet Dark. Night itself. The first vampire in the world. Unholy *merde*. . . .

Marmee Noir is part mystery, part dark, and thus the ultimate overwhelming enemy, and yet she is also the least tangible. Even less so than the long-distance psychic-phone-calling Belle Morte.

Marmee Noir first "wakes" and is introduced in *Cerulean Sins*, seemingly as a reaction to Belle Morte's amassing of forces and vampire politics machinations, but more likely in response to Anita herself. It appears that Anita's still-not-fully-tapped necromancer powers attract Marmee Noir like primeval elemental night attracts bats.

And that scary old bat—or at least her original mortal desiccated body—lies in a secret hidden chamber in an undisclosed location (possibly sharing the lair with Darth Vader and a certain former vice president). As she grows in self-awareness, she populates Anita's dreams as a more tangible presence, both vampire and prehistoric weretiger. Yes, that's how creepy-weird Marmee Noir is, both vampire and shape-shifter. With strangely perfumed wind effects. And jungle noises to mess with your mind.

Mostly, Marmee Noir is just plain old "Mommie Dearest," as Anita calls her: a straightforward elemental enemy and force of "supernature." Calling on the inner necromancer does not work to fight off the night. Instead, Anita uses Belle Morte's sexy *ardeur* gift to escape Marmee Noir's clutches; it's about the only thing that works against her. Sure, it's a mere distraction, but it's a useful one. This time, sex trumps death.

As Marmee Noir's presence continues growing like a super-weed and her psychic tendrils of awareness emerge into the world, it is also more difficult to fight her. But the vampires and others realize soon enough that *something* must be done. Modern weapons are used to blow up the chamber in which Marmee Noir's body lies. The explosion gets rid of her physical body, apparently destroying it, in *Skin Trade*. And yet, an indestructible psychic force, she "remains," and we can easily imagine her coming back like disembodied Voldemort from J. K. Rowling's *Harry Potter*, because power of such elemental scope and magnitude simply cannot be dissipated so easily, and Anita is not done with her.

In addition, the ability to call the great cats and ancient tigers and other heightened werepowers are a kind of perverse gift or "mark" from Marmee Noir, who has serious designs on both Anita's inner necromancer and panwere, and wants to possess Anita's body and come back to life in the modern day.

But where's the cooperation, you ask?

It's in the latter portion of *Skin Trade*. Marmee Noir reaches out to Anita and "asks" for her help, at the same time offering to fight their common dire enemy—Vittorio, once known as Father of the Day, the male counterpart of Marmee Noir, the one who's risen and is about to overtake the world.

For a brief instant, they are allies. Anita allows herself to surf the power of the ancient Night (ultimate deepest death) at the same time as she directs the *ardeur* against their common enemy. Thwarted sexuality, Vittorio's only weakness, works against him. (Here, I would say, Marmee Noir owes Belle Morte a box of blood chocolates.)

In the process of freely letting in and using both of her supernatural ally-enemies, Anita, the learning machine, enhances and unleashes her own personal power. Without thinking about it, she makes the enemies' forces her own.

Now who's the ultimate vampire?

Thus, four ally-enemies. Four faces of death. Two mortal ones she can *just barely* imagine defeating (Edward, Olaf), and two still beyond her, but definitely touchable with a ten-foot pole (Belle Morte, Marmee Noir).

But we can bet, as always, that Anita is underestimating her own potential.

Indeed, Anita Blake, Vampire Hunter, is a yet-unknown, ever-changing factor. With each book she goes deeper and further out, discovers new levels of personal darkness, her own unique flavor of power: the terrifying über-necromancer. It's the last, ultimate enemy she must conquer.

Ah, the self. . . .

Always seeing mirror aspects of herself in all the enemies she interacts with is a safe way of discovering and externalizing the many faces of Death and conquering it slowly, gradually, *safely* in herself. She finds it easier working with these others, the enemy, the impersonal mirrors, and just maybe learning more about her own darkness, secondhand.

Reflected in broken mirror shards are the sociopath, the murderer, the sadist, the empty thing, the lusting succubus, the necromancer, the vampire, the assassin, the executioner, the night itself. Death.

Which one is she? All of them, yes. Yet, which one is *truly* she?

Anita's enemy-ally All-Star Team is in fact a kind of kaleidoscopic multiple-personality phenomenon. It's as if she broke herself into several distinct personality "pieces" and laid then out before her like scary trump tarot cards to shuffle her own reading, her personal fate.

There goes The Tower, her Edward, a.k.a. certain Death, whose other face is faithful judgment.

Next in the Major Arcana, draw The Devil—convicted rapist and serial killer Olaf, master of the unfettered yet forbidden realm, able to unleash wild power over Anita.

Then comes The Lovers, dark and dual, in the beautiful face of Belle Morte, shimmering in the creative, sexual, generative promise.

Finally, the elemental force of Marmee Noir is The Chariot, rushing headlong into oblivion, yet on some level wielding perfect primeval control. . . .

As Anita deals each new enemy card, she remains in control also.

Because control is the last edge she has to push one day, the last line to cross all the way, without looking back. On the other side lies the mystery of self and the answer. Meanwhile, dealing these deadly "personality" team member cards is a way to procrastinate.

What about Anita's own personal trump card?

Why, it's Death, of course.

In Tarot, the Death card signifies not ultimate destruction, but *change* and the great *unknown*.

Will Anita ever face it?

The final revelations are yet to come.

◆　◆　◆

Vera Nazarian immigrated to the United States from the former USSR as a kid. She sold her first story when seventeen, has been published in numerous anthologies and magazines, seen on Nebula Awards Ballots, honorably mentioned in Year's Best volumes, and translated into eight languages.

A member of Science Fiction and Fantasy Writers of America, she made her novelist debut with the critically acclaimed *Dreams of the Compass Rose* (Wildside Press, 2002), followed by *Lords of Rainbow* (Betancourt & Company, 2003). Her novella *The Clock King and the Queen of the Hourglass* (PS Publishing, UK) made the *Locus* Recommended Reading List for 2005. Her collection, *Salt of the Air* (Prime Books, 2006, expanded and reissued by Norilana Books, 2009), contains the 2007 Nebula Award–nominated "The Story of Love." Recent work includes the 2008 Nebula Award–nominated fantasy novella *The Duke in His Castle* and the Jane Austen parody *Mansfield Park and Mummies*.

Vera lives in Los Angeles. In addition to being a writer and award-winning artist, she is also the publisher of Norilana Books. Visit her website: www.veranazarian.com.

I was interviewed by a sex therapist, for her radio show, who had a habit of guessing the backgrounds of her guests—off air, of course. She was almost always right, or at least in the ballpark. We talked and laughed and I answered questions on air. Afterward she judged from what I wrote and how comfortable I was with her questions and the call-in questions that I must have been raised in a very sexually comfortable household where information was freely shared. I had to tell her no. My grandmother taught me that sex was bad, my body was dirty, and men were evil and wanted only one thing, and that one thing would be unpleasant and they were animals to want it. Her advice before my first wedding was to lie back and it would be over soon. The radio show host was quiet for a moment and then she said, "You're remarkably healthy for your background."

Grandmother was a deeply unhappy woman, and tried her best to share that unhappiness with me. She gave me so little guidance that I turned to the library for sex information. I was the best-informed virgin in my high school, to the point where girls who were having sex came to me with questions. I have to say their unhappiness and lack of information after having had actual sex helped keep me uninterested in crossing that barrier until college. I educated myself through books not just about sex, but about the larger world outside the small rural town I lived in. I had no parents, no couple to emulate, and no marriage that I saw as happy around me, so I grew up free to remake that part of my socialization with very few preconceptions.

I didn't realize that my attitude toward sex, relationships, men and women interacting, was so different from societal norms until very late in life. I knew that men in college had trouble dating me more than once—or rather, that they and I came to a mutual agreement that one date was enough. I dated on my own terms, and saw no reason to compromise. I compromise better now than I did in college, but not on everything, and not ever on some things. That set me apart from most women, though I didn't know it, but what really set me apart and still does is my attitude toward sex and gender roles. First, I don't pigeonhole people by gender roles. My grandmother raised me to be the boy. Because she didn't have a man around the house, I was it. I value that because it meant I didn't think like a girl, or a boy, but as myself.

I still don't understand why everyone is weirded out by the sex in my books. Sex is normal; it's what we do for the species to survive, so why does it scare people so? Maybe it is the biologist in me, but I think it's also the fact that I had to create my own sexual identity with almost no help, because all the help offered me was negative. I rejected it. I would not be limited by such unhappiness, I would find my own way, and I did. I am now happily married and my husband, Jonathon, has no problem with the fact that I put the same time, attention, thought, and research into my real sex that I put into my fictional sex. My first husband was disturbed by the fact that I thought so much about it. He seemed to feel it should be natural and not so planned. Spontaneity is great, but *prior planning prevents poor performance* is not just a phrase for the military. I treat my sex life the way I treat all my life: carefully, with thoughtfulness, planning, goals, and a constant desire to improve my skill set. Jonathon has adopted my paradigm and thinks it works just dandy. It's nice to be with someone who thinks this is a plus and not a burdensome minus.

I didn't start out by trying to be the spokesperson for nonstandard sex, but the more people were upset by it, the more I thought, *Why?* Why is it such a hot button for people? I finally realized that one of the reasons people get so upset about the sex in my books is that it is nonstandard a lot of the time, and they're not upset because they didn't like reading the sex scenes, they're upset because they did like it. They're upset because this is maybe the first time they've ever read a BDSM scene and liked it, or read a group sex scene and liked it, or thought it would be nice to have that third adult in the house to help with all those daily chores.

The message of my writing is some version of this: that whatever it is, as long as you harm no one, not even yourself, you're okay. Whatever you want, whatever moves you, whatever makes your blood pump and your heart race is all good. There are no limits, so long as you harm none. Some have found that a very comforting message; others feel threatened by it. I meant it to be accepting and welcoming; the fear was not intended. But it's not fear of the unknown. I believe the negative reactions are so strong because what scares them is themselves and their reaction to what I write. I have no qualms about showing reality. Through my patina of monsters and magic, I get to jerk the covers back and show what's real and what's possible, whether that sheet being jerked back is in the bedroom or the morgue. I show the reader what is there, unflinching through the good, the bad, the complicated, and the scary. All the while I whisper, "It's okay. It's all right. Don't be afraid . . . of yourself."

—Laurell

Showing the Scars

JACOB CLIFTON

Every mystery story contains within it a secret that, when it is revealed, solves the equation of the story and puts the world right again. All the toys go back in their boxes until next time: Jessica Fletcher goes home to her Metamucil and six dozen cats; Phillip Marlowe goes out looking for a good-time girl and a bottle of rye; Sherlock and Watson have some tea. In its Modernist mode, the mystery story is set in a Rousseauist milieu, in which the world is naturally good, and the detective must assume the role of antibody: identifying the disrupting element and bringing it to justice, thus rebooting the world to its essential well-meaning roots.

Mystery, in its noir form, adds an existential twist, blurring this sense of good and evil and presenting a Hobbesian view of the world ("all against all") in which the detective is less antibody than victim of the Fates. Subsequent evolutions of the genre apply this uncertainty to the character of the hero himself: *The Shield*'s Vic Mackey is drawn into offenses against morality and legality Sherlock would find horrifying, and the protagonist of postmodern mysteries like *Memento* or Phillip Dick's novels finds that in fact he himself is the criminal.

In the new noir shape of mystery, from *Twin Peaks* to *The X-Files*, we find the presumptive antibody, the detective, implicated in the mysteries of the world rather than their modernist conqueror. The metaphor has transformed itself, from the personal drama of protagonist/reader as observer/problem-solver, returning the world to a state of grace, to an uncertain and open-ended exploration of self in dynamic relation to an ever-changing and often-confusing world. I would argue that this is a natural progression, in terms of our culture's view of itself and continually deepening attempts to interpret the confusion of the outside world by exploring the internal self.

The horror genre, which has found itself combined with every mode of mystery since before dear Edgar Allen, has followed a parallel path. The overpowering mojo of Bram Stoker's Dracula requires the protagonists to defend the sanctity of our natural world against its seductive, invading power; the Wolfman views his unfortunate condition as a curse; mummies and zombies don't even have voices or personalities, just irrepressible urges for destruction and terrifying, unnaturally animated movement.

Similar to the evolution[1] of the mystery genre, the horror movement of the late '70s turned a corner by letting us into the monster's head, and thus demonstrating the subjectivity of even the most horrific creature's existence. From poor Carrie White to the hapless *American Werewolf In Paris*, monsters were the new heroes—as long as we remembered, like the beekeeper or operator of a wolf sanctuary, that even the loveliest and most beloved of beasts can still bite. Hard.

There is another connection between the worlds of mystery and horror (and the latter's big sister, speculative fiction) essential to our discussion, which is the idea of internal rules. Every story (apart from the most self-consciously postmodern) has its background and logical rules, which must be followed in order for the mystery's conclusion to satisfy. No story suffers more from the *deus ex machina* than a mystery: imagine a story in which, after hundreds of pages, a heretofore unknown personage presents himself as the culprit, shocking detective and reader alike! Similarly, in order to retain any meaning, works of science fiction or horror must be made entirely of their

---

[1] I use "evolution" here only as a measure of the genre's ongoing transformation, not to suggest that worthwhile and enjoyable fictions aren't being written to this day using every mode available; after all, in postmodern fictions nothing is lost.

rules: they are the skeleton on which the entire story is built. A story about werewolves—and all the implicit themes that it brings to the table—cannot be resolved by alien abduction.

So we could say that, first, the development of genre fiction—mystery, science fiction, horror—shows a through-line of self-dissection: every writer wants to discover new territory, and report back to us what she finds, which means investigating the story's genre as much as its internal mystery. When dealing with such basic archetypes as the Vampire and the Shapeshifter, locating that new mythical territory means letting the genre question itself. If the first and most basic story construction is the classic man vs. nature plot with which we're all familiar, then all that follows that construction must involve somehow the systematic breaking down of that human/nature dividing line.

Secondly, it is important to remember that every story, if it's to generate revenue through publication, must be enjoyable and identifiable to the reader. We write the stories we want to read; the trick of success lies in those same stories also being those that *others* want to read. Fiction is a journey not only for the heroine and author, but for the reader herself. The challenge here is in adhering to genre rules without being constricted by them. It's a fine line, and one which any successful piece of genre writing must walk.

I contend that Laurell K. Hamilton's Anita Blake series is a postmodern work exploring these two particular lines of genesis—fulfilling the demands of both its genre and, commercially, satisfaction for the reader—and embracing them so wholeheartedly that the end product cannot help but be transgressive. By operating from her own fictional rules, and extrapolating them in line with her vision for the series and characters, Hamilton has created a complete world for readers to inhabit. She has also created a character whose changes, while sympathetically and lushly described, become more challenging and alien with every book. In fact, I would say Hamilton has created a subjective experience for an entirely new horror archetype: the Succubus. At this point in the series, it's fair to say that this sums up the series and Anita's development: from heroic "antibody," to antihero, to powerful monster in her own right.

Hamilton set out to create a wholly female counterbalance to the classic noir universe: a world in which, generally, the male hero is responsible for his own ethical decision-making; in which sex is a reward and sometime threat to his overall goals; in which neither author nor reader judges the detective for his behavior, language, or difficult and often violent choices. Extrapolating from these basic rules, we have Anita Blake in her original, Vampire Hunter form: a woman with identifiable neuroses, a personal creed of justice, a filthy mouth, and a willingness to negotiate with darkness. So far, so good, even as the final words in Anita's first adventure seem, to a modern audience, nothing less than a dare: "I know who and what I am. I am The Executioner, and I don't date vampires. I kill them."

But blustery hero rhetoric aside, Anita's femininity is a defining aspect of the character: she's not simply, in Marion Zimmer Bradley's immortal phrase, a "man with breasts." Her concerns are deeply female; her relationship to her monsters is emotional and romantic in a way that would make Phillip Marlowe weep. Her worldview is violent, powerful, and incapable of accepting gender imbalances that many of us might accept without question. Without being blind to the assumptions of others, Anita's public persona is built on an overriding strength: she is a workaholic competitor among competitors, not an overcompensating female in a world of males. This stance alone should provide notice that we are in a somewhat underutilized fictional space, in which the usual rules do not apply.

The millennium has provided us with an interesting new horror (and horror-romance) trope along these lines: stories about women of various character, beset by romantic and social entanglements with the twinned forces of seductive death (the Vampire) and terrifying life force (the Werewolf). Charlaine Harris's brilliant Southern Vampire series heroine, Sookie Stackhouse, bounces between suitors from both sides, as does Bella Swan in Stephenie Meyer's Twilight series. (Even the prodigiously brilliant Amelia Atwater-Rhodes split the difference, writing primarily about a vampire-witch war in one series—the Nyeusigrube stories—while developing a world of shapeshifters for her Kiesha'ra books.) Whatever the reasons for this fascinating new archetypal love triangle, Hamilton's greatest and most ambitious creation is a third, specifically and eternally female member of the trinity: the Succubus heroine.

Wherein lies the rub. While the Werewolf archetype developed originally out of superstitions about women, and women's blood and menstrual cycle particularly, and some of the earliest vampire stories (*Carmilla*, even *Dracula*) included great mythic content about these same fearful concepts, I would argue that both these archetypes—in the context of the new, heroine-centered literature described above—are relegated to symbols of male power, against which the female protagonist must define herself. Each of these bestselling series has found its own way of resolving this tension—eventually through the reevaluation or transformation of its heroine into a supernatural creature of her own—but the Anita Blake method is by far the most profound.

The Succubus is one horror archetype that is wholly and inescapably feminine, drawing on the deepest fears and nightmares of men and women alike. Though authors like Anne Rice have mined the myth of the Incubus (Rice in her Mayfair/Taltos stories), this archetype belongs to an altogether different order, more like the Vampire than a complement to it. The original succubus, Lilith of Judeo-Christian myth, consorted with demons at the beginning of time, and it so transformed her that she became a roving murderer of children, drawing upon the breath and life force of men as they slept.

In killing children, Lilith reverses primordial expectations of woman as nurturer; in raping men, she reversed perhaps the most basic principle of all. She is transgressive in every sense, and thus terrifying. Lilith serves a mythic role by representing men's own fears about their sexual prowess and control, as defined wholly against women's, in the same way that the werewolf metaphor so beautifully embodies loss of sexual and physical control in men—but without giving men a say in it! Lilith treats her victims as victims, objects, feeding on them to generate life within herself which she does not return to the world as offspring, and in this way refutes every ancient stricture placed on women.

In one story, Lilith was originally cast out of the Garden of Eden for presuming to take the dominant position in coitus with her husband, Adam, and everything that followed for her arises from this first transgression. (Compare the story of Eve, who made equal mistakes and assumptions, and earned the world's punishment just as efficiently. One almost wishes they'd made friends and taken the *Thelma & Louise* route—which I would say is where the mythic roots of that story actually begin!)

By developing the Succubus as a horror archetype through the development and transformation of her central character, Hamilton brings a burgeoning sense of dread and discovery that revitalizes Lilith's mythic power, making Anita's archetype every bit as intriguing and powerful an archetype as those of the vampires and shapeshifters that people her dark world. What's radical is the way in which Hamilton applies the very scientific attention to detail and authorial sympathy that makes her vampires and shapeshifters so compelling to her new monster. By giving that rigorous thought and detailed follow-through to an archetype based on destructive sexual hunger—putting her central character through these paces—Hamilton treads on the exposed nerve that the archetype itself embodies.

Anita's adventures are catalogued, from start to finish, through the eyes of a biologist, focused on the social and sexual constructs of humans who, under certain circumstances, physically become wolves or other carnivores. Apply that same dedication and deliberate description to the actions and experiences of a succubus, and you have the latter Anita books. Where the descriptive phrases regarding vampire activities must contain certain nouns, adjectives and verbs—hungers, bites, hypnotism, bleeding, slavery and mastery, etc.—and the words of werewolves are words of rage, hunger—that curious blend of violence and sensuality implicit in the phrase "Killing Dance"—it so follows that the semiotic web surrounding the archetype of the Succubus is going to include every possible word for sexual interaction.

Tedious or titillating—and the author seems to feel, with the reader, that they are both equally—these sexually descriptive passages are every bit as world-building and contributory as Hamilton's descriptions of a shapeshifter's physical transformation, or the precise hue of Nathaniel's eyes. They represent a direct translation of Anita's experience as she enters the world of monsters on her own terms, as a new kind of fearsome creature.

While this is, of course, terribly offensive for some readers and "negative fans," one is tempted to contrast the sexuality of Anita's later responsibilities with the lovingly detailed operations, protocols, and equipment generated in her incredibly violent work as "The Executioner"—or in the work of fan-favorite hired killer Edward, whose relationship with death and death-dealing is as graphic and sensual as Anita's relationships with her harem of men.

Sex is a huge part of Anita's world well before the *ardeur* enters the story. Anita herself seems mystified by the focus on sexual exploration among the vamps and hangers-on, even as Jean-Claude's attraction grows stronger and stronger. The *ardeur* is present in Jean-Claude's own vampiric bloodline, descending from the seductive Belle Morte, described as a unique ability *on the same neutral level* as that of the "rotting" vampires. If anything, this early parallel clarifies Hamilton's intent once Anita's own *ardeur* powers arrive. From the beginning, sex is notable among the monsters of Blake's world as a form of commerce, signaling political alliance, servitude, and personal currency as often as—or more than—it is displayed in more human terms of intimacy and affection. This too—treating sexuality logically and unemotionally—is in line with Hamilton's scientific predilections for understanding her creations, and in this schema, morality and gender roles are relegated to only minor roles. The sexual economy of Anita's world refuses to be distinguished from politics, industry, or the rest: they are all equal parts of the sociological machine.

Anita's political power grows, *Godfather*-like, with each novel, whether acquired sexually or otherwise. The accumulation of personal power in an uncertain world is a preoccupation of both the Anita Blake and Merry Gentry tales, and I believe it represents a feminist move toward overcoming the powerful hierarchies implicit in our society. It would be disingenuous at this point to avoid mentioning that sales of both series rise as the sexual escapades increase in volume and variety, but the point remains that the narrative worlds of Anita and Merry view sex and use of sexuality as means to an end, in addition to being an end in itself.

However, I would also mention a common symptom of all serial drama, whether on television or in comics or here in books, which is that the stakes must always be raised. Greater threats must be met with greater power, and *ardeur* aside I think Anita's impressive and non-stop accumulation of powers, roles, allies, and resources are a direct result of this commercial need. Anita's acquisition of each pard, pack, pride, power, triumvirate, mark, lover, and territory—they really do pile up quickly!—is necessary to meet the next awful thing, which is itself created to fulfill the reader's greater need for danger. Anita lives in such a dangerous world that to go without even one of her weapons—eventually, a collection that includes sex as literal power—would be deadly.

Which brings us back, again, to the rules of genre. Why is it that the *ardeur* is even necessary? Why can't Hamilton get rid of at least a few of the men in Anita's sexual compound? Why should the very plot of a novel depend on the workings of the *ardeur*, such as that plot-based necessity which explains the presence of Nathaniel *and* Micah, brought along on an Edward/Anita adventure and left for the most part in a hotel room, present only to feed Anita's need? Isn't it all, well, a bit cumbersome? I'm not being facetious when I point out that it is cumbersome having to sleep in a coffin, too. Turning into a half-crazed monster at the full moon is a real hassle. And poor over-endowed Micah, traumatized by the high school cheerleaders he's wounded in the past, well. . . .

Sex is a huge part of our world, and our lives, as well. It's often a hassle, it often substitutes itself for other virtues and activities, it is also used to wound, it is also used to accrue power. The difference is that we know better than to talk about it. Similarly, the violence implied by vampirism and lycanthropy, when connected to sexuality, leads directly and swiftly to some scary places. I think that the vampire-werewolf love triangle in current women's fiction speaks directly to a larger sexual trauma in our culture.

The vampire suitor is portrayed as courtly, protective, and simultaneously controlling and sinister: the very image of masculinity portrayed in the clichéd '90s Dartmouth feminisms in which women were taught, confusingly, both to demand sexual protection and to seek sexual freedom. For example, Jean-Claude's ambiguous power relationship with Anita is no less—in fact, a great deal more—frightening for feeling so *familiar*. To submit to Jean-Claude's vampiric influence, to the marks and mesmerism and mastery and the rest, would be no doubt satisfying—and masochistic—but would also subsume Anita's own personality and, at least in the earlier books, chosen identity.

Similarly, the animal suitor represents both a willingness and craving for sexual freedom, and the dangerous uncertainty that exists between men and women both physically and emotionally. To give in to Richard completely would entail accepting her own nature as a supernatural beast, surely; and later, the situation reverses itself, as Anita has so surpassed Richard that he becomes a would-be jailer, retreating from the shadow behind a picket fence of forced normality. And yet it is by focusing on Richard and Jean-Claude, with all their pitfalls and break up/make up circular phases, that Anita does her most important personal and sexual development.

The constant, queasy tension between Anita as an observer caught in the darkness (Jean-Claude, with his extensive network of weird friends and increasingly tense sexual history) and Anita as a dark creature caught in the world of grace (Richard's competing desires to somehow experience the world wholly as a beast, and lock that beast away forever) is an empirical portrayal of our integration of personal sexuality and public persona. Choosing Jean-Claude (and her eventual harem) means losing touch with the "real" world altogether, while choosing Richard means giving up on all that darkness—and all that sex!—in a double-bind familiar to anybody who ever questioned where the hell that word "slut" came from in the first place.

I believe that both archetypes, Vampire and Werecreature, are necessary, at this time in America, to work out the cultural traumas that result from our culture's shared history. In the last three generations alone we have experienced extreme gender oppression and extreme sexual freedom, resulting in a great deal of confusion and pain. I believe the vampire/animal/woman triumvirate in current fiction is an expression of our collective attempts to resolve these contradictions. Meyer's books construct these dangers as a metaphor for teen sexual fears, while Harris approaches the problem more directly, as a journey for her heroine's reclamation of her own body after historical sexual trauma.

Hamilton, however, again applies the existential rules of noir and pulp fiction to our wounded landscape. In Anita's world, sexual trauma is a matter of course—especially for men, which is another self-conscious reversal of the archetypes ("hooker with the heart of gold," "femme fatale," "daddy's little girl," "frigid/decadent virgin/whore") that represent womanhood in noir stories. Everybody has their kinks because everybody has a sexual history with mistakes in it, along a spectrum from the repressive personality (Richard!) to the deeply horrific (Edward's stepchildren). Hamilton's men (just as the women in Marlowe) comprise mainly sex workers and the sexually wounded. Anita's harem are physically smaller than the national average, putting them on a physical plane with Anita herself and reducing the natural intimidation a woman of her size would feel; they dress and behave in ways that are not always stereotypically male, some with hair down to their ankles. Their attitudes toward Anita's own growing power and insatiable needs are as forgiving and flexible as the nursemaid/whores that always show up just in time to hand Marlowe a gun.

But again, we see that instead of inverting a standard, frankly ugly and dehumanizing stereotype of woman-as-mindless object, Hamilton finds a way to strike a fresh balance. Most importantly, Hamilton's men come with their own baggage, often sad but never pitied, which must be lovingly and gently administered to and dealt with in order that life can continue. Their business becomes Anita's, becomes ours, and more than anything becomes one of the parts of the Hamilton biologist's machine. I think it's courageous, frankly, to address such touchy subjects as bondage, rape, and sadomasochism respectfully, as consequences of our history, while still accepting them as issues not to be ignored or denigrated. While a guilt-free, pain-free, shame-free sexuality might be a part of the world of grace, it's unlikely that any of us have sufficiently escaped our history to the degree that it's possible. By acknowledging the history that leads to the harem's various sexual proclivities—and by avoiding the genre's recent BDSM bravado, which seeks above all to deny even the possibility of historical or psychological elements in those proclivities—Anita (and Hamilton) gives these men the freedom to express their own sexuality unburdened by fear.

In this case, Anita does so both by her nonjudgmental attempts to take their emotional and sexual needs into consideration (I'm thinking here specifically of Anita's forcing herself to be cognizant of Nathaniel's submissive needs, which are openly regarded as a symptom of earlier trauma, or her open-armed leap into Jean-Claude's complex relationship with Asher, both of which represent active transgression of her own sexual boundaries for the sake of love), and by responding to her growing harem not as a typical male hero would (by containing them all in a room full of pillows and incense, virtue guarded by eunuchs) but as a real woman might: by trying to contain her jealousy, and swiftly learning that nonstop sex requires a serious amount of logistical oversight! Only a woman with a seriously pragmatic sense of humor could possibly write a wish-fulfillment sex fantasy that involves quite so much worrying over laundry and getting everybody fed and cleaned and bedded down each night with a kiss to the forehead. One is reminded of an XXX Neverland, in which Wendy spends as much time laughing to herself as she spends calming distraught Lost Boys down after a big tiring day.

In fact, it's in this attention to consequences that Hamilton's obsession with detail and playing by her narrative rules comes most closely into focus. For a book ostensibly about—and full of—chapter-long, intensely detailed, multiple-partner, multiple-orgasm, multiple-position, often painful (or at best unlikely to be pleasurable), frankly *exhausting* sex, it certainly came as a surprise to yours truly to read my first Anita book, *Danse Macabre*, and discover that it begins with a seriously long (and hilarious) discussion among approximately fifteen people about the children that might result from such a wild sequence of events: the fictional medical complications that might result, the touchiness of assigning paternity, the volunteering for daycare and nightly care, the soothing of ruffled feathers and raised hackles over all the larger implications, the communal household complications of the pregnancy, the belabored scheduling of said sexual romps, etc. In fact, I was delighted. I don't read a lot of porn, but I've *never* read porn that worried over the details and consequences of what is essentially considered a delightful activity even slightly, much less in such meticulous depth.

And, of course, we mustn't forget that *ardeur* is French for *le total hassle for everybody*. Again, only the most pragmatic sense of humor would seek to imbue supernatural significance to that sinking feeling we've all felt, coming home after a long, awful day at work only to be surprised by that certain gleam in a loved one's eye. But Hamilton has already, throughout the series, unhinged sex from its usual signifiers by making it a purely biological and magical act. No matter how many *National Geographic* videos of animals mating you watch—lions, tigers, hyenas—you're never going to see a single candlelit dinner, good red wine, foot rubs, favorite novels or poetry, or any of the other tokens that get human animals laid.

In the biological, animal kingdom of which Hamilton is a devoted student, mating is part of the job. We hunt or scavenge, we mate, and we care for our young. We help out Darwin by doing two things well: not dying, and having kids. There's no dating, no breakups, and no making up. There's barely even any commitment beyond the few minutes necessary: just the need, from deep incomprehensible places, being met by the best possible nearby option. Which is to say that the attraction between animals is closer to the *ardeur*, shaping the behavior and attitudes of our best possible mates through magical, rather than biological means—or, science would say (though we hate to listen), through our own behavior—than it is to the human constructs and social niceties that obscure it. *Ardeur*, on a sufficiently large scale, is not that different from the forces and weirder effects generally ascribed to evolutionary law. Watching those animals on TV isn't disturbing because it's so alien; it's disturbing because we recognize, on a basic level, what they're up to.

So we see the ways in which Hamilton makes Anita's succubus duties every bit as important and demanding as those of Necromancer Anita, or U.S. Marshal Anita, or Detective Anita. I think the disconnect between book and reader, when it occurs, takes place at the line where sexuality becomes purely about commerce or currency. The moral majority in America would proudly explain that it is scared to death of looking at sex as anything other than the loving and committed expression of physical affection between a legally married man and woman, above the age of consent and giving it willingly, for the purposes of procreation. As our hypothetical representative sample becomes more and more liberal in its sexual morality, individual words and qualifications disappear from that sentence, but most would draw the line at *some* point in there. Yours is probably different from mine, but not so much so that we would come to blows.

What Hamilton has done—with the rules she's set for herself as a writer (about the kind of woman and heroine Anita must be) and the rules she has set for her world (a purely Hobbesian free-for-all in which sex, death, violence, and love circle each other the same boxing ring, constantly bleeding and constantly making up)—is *remove that line entirely*. Terrifying, simply horrifying. In a horror novel. How . . . novel!

As exercises in world-building logic, as exercises in reviving old mythical tropes and giving them new and raucous life, as exercises in feminist reinvention of more recent horror and mystery tropes, and as judgment-free surveys of sexual and romantic possibilities—and scary certainties!—the *ardeur* as a motivating force and Anita's ascendance as a female monster out of myth can be considered organic extrapolations from first principles.

All writers have one goal: to speak, to be heard, to communicate personal complexities of emotion and experience. Writers do one thing only: reach out through the page to touch the reader and say, "There. Now we are both less alone."

This essay takes its title from an incident in *Bloody Bones* in which Anita puts a victim of vampire attack at ease by showing him her own scars. I think that by showing the considerable toll, and often awkward or painful methods, of Anita's ongoing transformation into a creature of the night, the ongoing story elevates itself beyond simple sensationalism. I think that by showing the emotional and physical impact our personal and sexual histories have on our present lives and our relationships, Hamilton is seeking an honest portrayal of the more shadowed parts of our culture. And I think that through her own vulnerability and honesty as an author—a human being not much unlike any other humans you've met in your life—and by honoring the painful lives and prices of Anita and her thousand lovers in Anita's ongoing survival, Hamilton seeks to put us at ease in just that way. After all, I would say it's the mandate of the horror writer most of all to say the scariest thing imaginable, the better to reach through the page and touch the reader, and simply say:

"I'm scared, too. We're in this together."

◆   ◆   ◆

Jacob Clifton is a novelist and staff writer for Television Without Pity and the Science Channel's *Remote Possibilities*. He spends nights revising his novels *The Urges* and *Mondegreen*, and his days wishing Team Bella were a viable alternative.

About Laurell K. Hamilton

Paranormal thriller writer Laurell K. Hamilton is the #1 *New York Times* bestselling author of two series. The first Anita Blake, Vampire Hunter novel, *Guilty Pleasures*, was published in 1993. There are now more than 6 million copies of Anita in print worldwide, published in sixteen languages. As the series approaches nineteen novels, with *Flirt* and *Bullet* being released in February and June 2010, Anita Blake only continues to grow in power and popularity. *A Kiss of Shadows* introduced Merry Gentry, a Fey Princess of the Unseelie Court and Los Angeles Private Investigator. With eight novels in the series, sales for the Merry Gentry books now exceed 2 million copies.

Hamilton currently resides in St. Louis with her husband, daughter, and pampered pug. She invites you to visit her website at www.laurellkhamilton.org or follow her on Twitter under @LKHamilton.

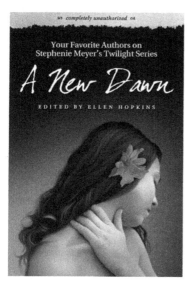

so *completely unauthorized* ca

Your Favorite Authors on
Stephenie Meyer's Twilight Series

A New Dawn

EDITED BY ELLEN HOPKINS

Love Twilight?

A New Dawn
Your Favorite Authors on
Stephenie Meyer's Twilight Series

Edited by Ellen Hopkins

Join some of your favorite writers as they look at the series with fresh eyes, and fall in love with Bella and Edward, and their world, all over again.

- ✄ Is Edward a romantic or a (really hot) sociopath?
- ✄ What does Bella and Edward's relationship say about free will?
- ✄ Who would you rather date: the guy who thirsts for your blood, or the guy who drinks out of the toilet?

With essays by Megan McCafferty, Cassandra Clare, Rachel Caine, and many more!

Available everywhere October 2009

Read an excerpt at TeenLibris.com!

Printed in the United States
by Baker & Taylor Publisher Services